# CalmingCrafts

# CalmingCrafts

relaxing crafts to inspire your creativity

by Dawn Frankfort

BRISTOL PUBLISHING ENTERPRISES, INC.

San Leandro, California

Design: Kari Ontko, India Ink

Photography: Lisa Keenan

Illustrations: Shanti Nelson

Project Editor: Lisa M. Tooker

Production: Kristen Wurz

Printed in Hong Kong through Global Interprint,
Santa Rosa, California.

contents

# Introduction

We live in a busy society. Many of us are balancing families and careers, while also trying to keep in touch with friends. If there is one word that is lacking in our lives, it is time. There is simply too little of it. When you look at everything you do in your life and the things you do for others, there is always someone who gets left out or does not get the attention he or she deserves. That someone is you.

While we may try to be creative during the little time we have, when we really look at what we actually do that is creative, we find that area of our life to be sparse. Besides the time factor, unless you took classes in school, you may have never learned how to create candles or other objects. Yet, if you're like so many others, you always wanted to try.

*Calming Crafts* was written especially for those of us who have always wanted to pursue something creative, but didn't know how.

The results of my crafts, from an *Eye Pillow* to a *Rosebud Poured Wax Candle* to *Peppermint Body Bar* soap to *Tropical Paradise* potpourri to fountains were picked for their relaxation properties. These easy-to-make pursuits represent new kinds of craft — crafts that calm. Crafts with an end result designed to allow you to rest, relax and renew.

*Calming Crafts* can be pursued alone or with friends and family. Each craft is designed to bring out the artist within, using colors and scents. The crafts also have built in meditation time. Whether stirring the soap, filling the pillows, melting the wax, blending the botanicals or building the fountain — each endeavor is designed to provide a sense of balance.

You can begin with any of the chapters that interest you. All follow a specific pattern. Each begins with a main recipe and is followed by variations of that theme. Sit back in a comfy chair, enjoy a latte or a herbal tea and relax. Here's to the enjoyment of crafts and time for you!

—*Dawn Frankfort, San Francisco 1999*

## Acknowledgments

Writing this book involved the help of many people. Each chapter had a sort-of mentor who was helpful with advice, information and/or supplies. I'd like to thank Tom Yaley, from Yaley Enterprises who was generous with advice, as well as candle wax and supplies; Jeff Vandel, of James Farrell & Co., for advice and buckwheat hulls and flaxseeds; Harry Hull from H2B Company, for his helpful advice on pillows; Bret Morat of Morat's Fine Hand-Crafted Soaps for his insightful and inspired words of wisdom about soap; Susan Picklesheimer and Diane Zack of FountainHeads for their advice on fountains; and Neil Hanscomb of San Francisco Herb Co., for his wisdom on potpourri.

On a personal note, I'd like to thank my family, Robyne, Bob and Alex Howard, Heidi, Bob and Jordan Keyes, Amy Shavelson, Cody and Sasha. And friends and helpful souls along the way, including Fred Maslin, B.L . Ochman, Mary Fetherolf, Kathy Hennessey, Mindy Sitzer, Jeannie Griego, Diane Walker, Ginger Jordan, Cally Griffith, Jackie Rogoff and Sheryle Baker.

Miss you, Mom, Russell, Natalie, Shirley, Bob and Jerry.

KODAK EPY 6018    52    51    91

# candles

Live what you believe—
make your whole life your art.

— SUE BENDER

While I love all the calming crafts in my chapters equally, I must admit that making candles is special. Candles provide not only illumination, but warmth and ambiance. The glow from the flame of a candle in a darkened room and the presence of someone you love is very romantic. Candles bring a sense of comfort, reassurance and warmth into our homes.

The pleasure and joy I get from making candles has absolutely surprised me. One of the things I most love about candles is that once you have learned the basic formulas, there are endless varieties you can make. By adding simple ingredients, you can blend scents, change a candle's texture or create unique designs.

The making of candles also provides an overall release of stress from a hectic day. The breaking up of wax blocks bangs away the tension, literally! I love the nurturing aspects of melting and stirring the wax and the craftsman-like quality of pouring it into a mold. The end product will bring out the artist in you. You'll find that the description of making candles is in two words — simply wonderful. I hope you enjoy it as much as I do.

## Scents

A scented candle can add a special feeling to a room. Certain scents are said to enhance moods, ease tension and create a feeling of overall well-being.

For best results when making poured candles, use candle fragrance made from a candle manufacturer. Concentrated candle scent blocks work particularly well and are more cost-effective than liquid candle scents or pure essential oils. The candle scents are highly concentrated and specially formulated to achieve optimum results. After the wax has been completely melted and the proper temperature achieved, the candle fragrance should be stirred into the wax just before pouring it into the mold.

For rolled beeswax candles, soak the wick in alcohol-free essential oils and then roll the wax sheet tightly around it. Let the essential oils dry for about an hour before lighting the candle. Or, use an eye dropper to place essential oil on the outside of the wax, let it absorb for about 30 minutes, and then you're ready to enjoy your freshly scented candle.

## Candle molds

I can speak from experience when I say that you're probably going to love candle molds. Choose molds that appeal to your creative instincts. Molds come in every shape imaginable. The more popular shapes include cylindrical, rectangular, square, oblong, star and triangular. Molds are generally made of metal, plastic or rubber. My favorite molds are made of metal because they are longer-lasting. (I used metal molds for all of the poured wax candle recipes in this chapter.)

A metal mold will come with a screw, a small strip of putty, a dowel and wicking. The screw and dowel hold the wick taut in the middle of the mold so it will stay together when the hot wax is poured into the metal container. The screw and putty also provide a seal so the hot wax does not come through the hole at the bottom of the mold. Prices run $15 to $25.

Polycarbonate candle molds are seamless and quite strong, but will not hold as much wax as a metal mold. They come in a variety of shapes and sizes, akin to metal molds. Prices average $20 to $30.

Plastic molds usually are in the shape of animals or flowers. They tend to hold lighter amounts of wax and are not as long-lasting as metal and hard plastic molds. Prices run $6 to $12.

## Candlewicks

When you buy molds, you will find that a string of wick, enough for several candles, is generally included. Wick varies from manufacturer to manufacturer. Wicks come in small, medium and large sizes. The appropriate size is based on the diameter, not the height of a candle. A small wick is used for votives or petite disk candles, less than 2 inches. A medium-sized wick is generally used in candles 3 to 4 inches in diameter. A large wick is used for candles 5 inches or wider.

• • •

Create a nightly bath ritual. Fill the tub with water infused with bath oils, crystals and bubbles. Light one of your handmade candles, place it by the tub and turn off the lights. Sit back and luxuriate in the warmth of the water and be bathed by the candle's warm glow. Close your eyes and let the problems of the day drift away. Breathe in the subtle scents from the candle's flame. Relax. Ahead is a gentle sleep. Tomorrow brings the promise of a new day.

Two kinds of wicks work well in poured candles: wire-core wicks or bleached wicks (bleached wicks do not have metal cores).

For rolled beeswax candles use only a bleached wick, or the candle will burn too hot or quickly.

## Candle wax

When pouring candles, use paraffin wax. You'll find several well-established manufacturers who make candle wax and candle-making equipment in the *Suppliers Resource List* on page 124.

What separates one kind of paraffin wax from another is its melting point. A melting point is determined by the amount of oil within the wax. If the wax is high in oil, a lower temperature is needed, such as 140° to 165°F. Wax with less oil will melt at a higher temperature of 160° to 185°F. The desired temperature should be listed on the packaging of your purchased wax. If a recommended temperature is not listed, use 190°F as an average temperature and never exceed 210°F.

If you're using a soft wax with a low flash point and melting point, you must melt the wax in a container of hot water to avoid a fire or an explosion. Using a container to melt wax also keeps cleaning to a minimum.

NOTE

Sometimes when candles are burned and the flame is extinguished, you will notice a small rolled-up ball at the wick's end. There is nothing wrong with the candle; the ball simply means your candle burned too fast. Before the candle is used again, snip off the ball with a pair of scissors and your candle will be fine.

Candle wax can be found in blocks from 1 pound to 20 pounds on average. Certain manufacturers make wax for specific molds and candle types. A premium wax is best for making molds for poured candles.

You'll have to break the wax apart since it comes in blocks. It sounds like hard work, but it's actually a fun part of the process and perfect after a hard day. Simply place the wax in a cardboard box, and using a screwdriver as a chisel, start banging away with a hammer. The resulting wax pieces should be no more than 2 inches around for quicker melting. It's a great workout and wonderful for clearing the mind!

While candle making is one of the best things you can do to relax, you are working with fire, so please be cautious. Never leave a pot of melting wax on the stove unattended. If the phone rings or your attention is taken away from the pot, first turn off the stove, move the pot to a cool burner and then answer the phone. Watch the temperature closely and never melt wax at a higher temperature than recommended by the wax manufacturer.

### Candle additives

Opaque crystals will add a cloudy quality and a pastel tint to the wax. Translucent crystals will make the candle appear clearer.

### Cleaning candle molds

While rubber or plastic molds can be washed with water, it is best to use a cleaning solution for metal molds, which can be found at hobby stores. Another great way to clean a metal mold is to line a cookie sheet with tin foil, place the mold upside down on the tin foil and stick it in the oven on a low temperature. Wax pieces should melt and drip out of the candle mold and onto the foil. Do not exceed 4 minutes, or the metal might warp.

| PROJECT TIP | Erasing Candle Flaws

*If there are too many air bubbles in your candles,* then you're probably pouring the wax too quickly. Next time pour more slowly. Always remember that after pouring, you need to gently tap the mold on all sides to release the air bubbles.

*If the candle folds into itself when burning,* then the wick size is likely too small. When you make another candle, use the next larger wick size.

*If the candle has fractures,* then the cause is generally related to cold temperature. It could mean that the mold,

particularly if it is made of metal, was cold, the room temperature was too warm or too cool, or the wax was too cold when poured. Always remember that for candles to set properly, they need to be poured in a room with an average temperature of 60° to 70°F. The melting point also needs to be around 190°F. If the metal mold feels cold, then warm the inside and outside of the mold with a hairdryer for a couple of minutes.

*If the candle has too many pit marks,* then the wax was likely poured too quickly, the temperature was too high or the mold had residual wax inside.

## General Materials and Tools

*premium wax*

*candle-making molds, preferably metal*

*metal core or bleached medium-sized wick*

*candle color dye chips or blocks, optional*

*concentrated candle scent blocks or 100% pure essential oils*

*newspapers*

*1 candle or candy thermometer*

*1 Pyrex pouring pitcher with spout or a metal container with pouring spout*

*1 wooden or metal spoon*

*2 to 4 aluminum, disposable cake pans (found in the cooking section of the grocery store)*

*1 (8 gallon) stainless steel non-Teflon pot*

*1 food scale*

*1 strip of putty (usually included in candle mold)*

*1 dowel (usually included in candle mold) or pencil*

*1 cardboard box*

*1 hammer*

*1 screwdriver*

*1 acrylic cutting board*

*1 pair of scissors*

*1 paring knife*

*1 vegetable peeler*

## Poured Wax Candles: Main Recipe

This candle literally sets the mold for the rest of the poured wax candles that follow. What I really love about this candle is that it is easy to make and the results are fabulous. Within a matter of hours you have something beautiful and functional that you made with your own hands.

NOTE: The following directions are to be used as the main directions for all the poured wax candle recipes. When needed, specific directions will be included for each recipe. Before attempting recipes with specific directions, please review the main recipe first.

store cost: $20 to $40

handmade cost: Under $10

Depending on the size, type and complexity of the candles you are making, investment in supplies and tools will vary. METAL MOLDS run around $15 to $25, but with proper care can be reused for years. WAX costs vary: a 4-pound slab runs around $14, and makes about 4 candles (3-inch x 4-inch each); an 11-pound slab costs around $20 and makes 11 to 12 candles. COLOR TABS cost approximately $2 and will make at least 8 to 16 candles, depending on size. CONCENTRATED CANDLE SCENT BLOCKS are $2 and will also make 8 to 16 candles, depending on size. You might also choose to buy liquid

candle scents; however, this costs twice as much and will make fewer candles. For the savings, I prefer candle blocks. WICKS cost about $2 and include about 6 feet per package. Each package makes 15 to 20 candles, depending on size. *Note:* To really save money, buy in bulk wholesale from the manufacturer and save anywhere from 25 to 50% off retail prices.

<u>time</u>: About 2 hours, plus a minimum of 6 hours to cool

### INGREDIENTS

*15 ounces premium wax*
*5 inches metal core wick or bleached wick*
*5 to 8 shavings color, or 1/8 ounce of a color block*
*5 to 8 shavings concentrated candle scent block, or 1/8 ounce scent block, or*
   *10 to 12 drops essential oil*

### MOLD

*3-inch x 4-inch-round cylinder metal mold*

### DIRECTIONS

#### PREPARE A WORK AREA

1. Since you will be working by the stove, use a kitchen table or a nearby counter free from cool drafts to set up your work area. Layer newspapers over the table or counter area and floor to prevent wax drip stains.

2. Keep the area warm by turning up the heat to 60° to 70°F as candles set up best in warm rather than cool temperatures.

3. Near the stove have a thermometer, pouring pitcher, spoon, cake pans, pot and scale ready.

#### PREPARING WICK IN MOLD

1. Turn the metal mold over. You will see a hole in the bottom of the mold.

2. Thread the wick from the bottom to the top of the mold.

3. Leave 1 inch of wick at the bottom, wrap once around the screw head and tighten.

4. Pull the wick tight.

5. Flatten putty over the screw to prevent wax from seeping out.

6. Lay a dowel across the top of the mold.

7. At the top of the mold, wrap the wick tight once around the dowel. Cut away excess wick.

8. Place the mold on a flat surface.

#### CHOPPING WAX

1. Place a block of wax in a cardboard box. Using a hammer and a screwdriver as a chisel, chop the block into approximately 2-inch chunks.

*Note:* The smaller the chunks, the quicker they will melt. You can use larger chunks, but they will take longer to melt.

2. Place a bowl on a scale and reset the measuring device to zero. Add chunks to the bowl until you have 15 ounces of wax. (If you do not have a scale that can be reset to zero, weigh the bowl and add the bowl's weight to the wax.)

## MELTING WAX

1. Place chopped wax in an 8-gallon metal pot. If soft wax, place a container of wax in a pot of boiling water.

2. Turn the burner on the stovetop to medium-high heat.

3. With a spoon, slowly stir the wax until all the chunks are melted.

4. Place the thermometer in the pot.

5. When the temperature reaches 190°F, turn off the heat, add color and slowly blend until the shavings have completely dissolved.

6. Add candle fragrance or essential oil and stir slowly for about 30 seconds until the scent is completely mixed.

## POURING WAX

1. Slowly pour the wax into a pitcher.

2. Tilt the mold slightly and slowly pour the wax into the mold. Fill the mold to about 1/4 inch from the top. Pour the extra wax back into the pot.

3. Gently tap the mold on all sides to free air bubbles.

## SETTING WAX

1. Leave the mold undisturbed, free from sudden movement.

2. After 45 minutes to 1 hour, you will notice a crevice or a hole around the wick area. Do not be alarmed; this is caused by the wax contracting and is normal and expected.

3. To allow the wax to breathe, take a pencil and poke a hole on either side of the wick. Thickened wax should be revealed. If liquid comes up, wait another 30 minutes and poke again until the wax is not fluid, but thick and mushy.

4. To refill the hole, heat the remaining wax in a pot at 160°F; only a small amount of wax should be needed.

5. Pour the wax into a pitcher.

6. Pour the wax into the crevice until it meets the original wax line.

7. After 1 hour, another crevice may form. Continue to repeat steps 3 through 6 until you no longer see a crevice.

8. Let the mold set for at least 6 hours.

FREEING WAX FROM MOLD

1. Remove the putty and screw.

2. Dislodge the dowel from the top. Turn the mold upside down.

3. The candle should easily slide out. If the candle does not slide out, gently tap all around sides.

4. If the candle still does not easily slide out, place it in the freezer for about 5 minutes.

5. The candle should slide out. If you still have trouble, stick it in the freezer for 2 more minutes (you might get a few cracks, but you'll free the candle).

6. Viola!

## Layered Poured Wax Candle

store cost: $12 to $30

handmade cost: Under $10

time: 8 to 10 hours

SPECIAL INGREDIENTS

*1³⁄₄ pounds premium wax*
*3 to 4 shavings forest green color*
*3 to 4 shavings cranberry color*
*¹⁄₈ block eucalyptus concentrated candle scent, or 10 to 12 drops eucalyptus essential oil*

MOLD

*2³⁄₄-inch x 6¹⁄₂-inch square metal mold*

SPECIAL DIRECTIONS

1. Melt half of the wax chunks in a pot. Add green color shavings.

2. Slowly pour the wax into the mold. The mold should be just under half full.

3. After 45 minutes to 1 hour, poke holes around the wick to allow the wax to breathe.

4. Reheat wax and pour to fill the crevice. Let the candle stand for 45 minutes to 1 hour.

5. If a crevice still appears, then poke additional holes around the wick, reheat the wax and fill the hole again, and let stand for 45 minutes to 1 hour at 160°F.

6. Put the remaining wax in the pot and melt.

7. Add cranberry shavings. Slowly pour the wax into the candle mold.

8. Repeat steps 5 through 8.

9. Allow the candle to set for at least 6 hours and then remove it from the mold.

10. Marvel at your creation!

• • •

While you can use any size candle mold to make candles, I think the layered candle in a taller mold has a particularly striking effect. I've chosen the colors green and cranberry with a eucalyptus scent, but you may select any colors or scent you like. You may also choose to use an unscented candle. The object here is to layer two or more colors together in a single candle. This candle takes more time and effort than a basic poured wax candle, but the result is well worth it.

This is a trendy and fashionable look for a candle. Yes, believe it or not, candles have style! Some of the patterns in this candle resemble snowflakes. They are formed when mineral oil is added to the heated wax. The patterns can look quite intricate and preplanned, but in fact, they are unique and spontaneous. The mineral oil adds white patterns to whatever color candle you choose. If you want a less intricate look, add less mineral oil. Experiment with the amounts to achieve your desired candle. In this recipe, I have chosen a red candle. One of the reasons I love this candle so much is because the patterns are artistic and give the candle an interesting look.

This is a very impressive candle, the one that will illicit the most "oohs and aahhhs" from family and friends. When lit, this candle is reminiscent of light shining through stained glass. The different colored chunks of wax are embedded in clear wax. This colorful candle is my personal favorite because it is dramatic and intricate, yet it is easy to make.

# Marbleized Poured Wax Candle

store cost: $12 to $30

handmade cost: $10 or under

time: 6 to 8 hours

SPECIAL INGREDIENTS
*5 to 8 shavings red color*
*¼ cup mineral oil*

MOLD
*2½-inch x 3½-inch x 4-inch oval-shaped metal mold*

SPECIAL DIRECTIONS

1. Melt approximately 10 ounces of wax chunks in a pot.

2. Add red color shavings and mineral oil.

3. Slowly pour the wax into the mold.

4. After 45 minutes to 1 hour, poke holes around the wick to allow wax to breathe.

5. Reheat the wax to 160°F and pour to fill the crevice.

6. Let the candle stand for 45 minutes to 1 hour.

7. If another crevice appears, then poke additional holes around the wick, reheat the wax and fill the hole again.

8. Let the candle stand for a minimum of 6 hours. Release the candle from the mold.

# Chunk Poured Wax Candle

store cost: $20 to $40

handmade cost: Under $10

time: 8 to 10 hours

CHUNK AND CANDLE INGREDIENTS
*3 pounds wax*
*5 to 8 shavings each of 3 colors*
*1 pound premium wax*

MOLD
*3¾-inch x 9½-inch five-point star metal mold*

*[ Makes enough chunks for at least 2 candles. ]*

1. Melt 1 pound of wax.

2. After the temperature of the wax reaches 190°F, add shavings of 1 color.

3. Pour the wax into a cake pan. Repeat steps 1 through 3 for each of the remaining 2 colors.

4. Allow the wax to set. To speed up the process after the wax begins to set and is still warm to the touch, place the mold in the freezer for less than 1 hour or until it sets completely. (There may be cracks, but that is okay since the chunks will be scored, embedded in the wax and the flaws hidden.)

5. Remove the wax from each cake pan; it will easily slip out in a block. Place it on a clean surface such as an acrylic cutting board.

6. With a ruler and a paring knife, score the wax into 1-inch x 1-inch blocks.

7. Cut the wax into chunks with a paring knife. You'll likely find that the chunks may not be uniform, but that is fine. The irregular shapes contribute to the overall look of the candle. Use a variety of forms or make them similar. Repeat for each color.

8. Fill the mold from bottom to top with colored chunks. Spread evenly into the points of the star mold.

9. Heat 1 pound of premium wax and pour it into the mold over the colored chunks.

# Confetti Poured Wax Candle

store cost: $12 to $30

handmade cost: $3 to $4

time: 6 to 8 hours

SPECIAL INGREDIENTS

*5 ounces candle shavings and pieces*
*10 ounces premium candle wax*
*5 to 8 shavings strawberry concentrated candle scent block, or 10 to 12 drops*
*strawberry essential oil*

MOLD

*3-inch x 4-inch-round cylinder metal candle mold*

HOW TO CREATE CANDLE SHAVINGS AND PIECES

1. Choose at least 3 colors of extra wax. I used red, light green and purple in the recipe, but you can choose any three or more colors you like.

2. Using a vegetable peeler, shave off small strips of wax from each candle.

• • •

Like many things, candles are recyclable. I found this out when I decided to do something with my extra candle wax. This recipe is the result.

In random places, the colored wax shavings and small pieces of candle resemble confetti encased in clear wax. The wax takes on pastel tones from the wax chips. At the top of the candle the shavings and pieces look like speckles of shiny glass. This provides an interesting textural contrast to the matte finish of the candle.

3. For contrast, also use a paring knife to cut off small pieces of candles so they resemble tiny chunks, about a $\frac{1}{8}$-inch diameter. Keep colors in separate piles.

SPECIAL DIRECTIONS

1. In the round candle mold, layer 1 inch of green shavings and pieces.

2. Layer 1 inch of red shavings and pieces.

3. Layer 2 inches of purple shavings and pieces.

4. Melt clear wax to 190°F.

5. Add strawberry scent.

6. Pour just enough wax into the mold to cover and set the shavings and pieces.

7. Allow the candle to set for 10 minutes.

8. Reheat the clear wax to to 160°F, and pour the remaining wax $\frac{1}{4}$ inch from the top of the mold.

9. Sprinkle any additional shavings and pieces of colored wax on top of the mold.

10. Allow the candle to set for 6 or more hours.

## Decorated Candles

Now that you know how to pour candles into different shapes and sizes, you might want to try decorating candles, too. These candles have an earthy, natural look and are simple to make. Just take a basic poured candle, choose a scent and adhere different materials including leaves, herbs, fruits and flowers to the outside of the candle.

Fallen leaves can become treasures when added to the wax of a candle. Some herbs also offer impressive leaves like those found on lemon verbena. I'm using green wax and green leaves, but you can choose any color wax or leaves of different colors if you'd like.

## Leaf Poured Wax Candle

store cost: $15 to $30

handmade cost: $3 to $5

time: 3 hours

SPECIAL TOOLS
*1 old bowl*
*1 small paintbrush or makeup brush*

SPECIAL INGREDIENTS
*dry leaves gathered from outdoors to cover the candle*
*8 to 10 ounces wax*
*4 to 5 shavings lemon concentrated candle scent block, or 5 to 6 drops lemon essential oil*
*1 basic poured wax candle*

1. Gather dried tree or herb leaves. For this candle, I'm using lemon verbena leaves from my garden.

2. Melt the colored wax completely. Add scent to the wax.

3. Pour the wax into a bowl.

4. Dip a brush into the wax, paint the wax on a leaf and quickly press it on the candle. Add more wax if needed for adherence. Repeat for each leaf.

5. As the wax cools, you will have to quickly reheat and apply the wax to the leaves.

6. Reheat the remaining wax.

7. Pour wax over the entire outside of the candle. Allow wax to run down the leaves. This creates an interesting effect and helps ensure that the leaves stick to the candle.

8. Allow the candle to set for 2 hours.

## Fruit Poured Wax Candle

store cost: $15 to $30

handmade cost: $4 to $6

time: 3 hours

SPECIAL TOOLS
*1 old bowl*
*1 small paintbrush or makeup brush*

SPECIAL INGREDIENTS
*dehydrated orange slices to cover the candle*
*8 to 10 ounces wax in the same color as the candle*
*4 to 5 shavings orange concentrated candle scent block, or 5 to 6 drops orange*
  *essential oil*
*1 basic poured wax candle*

SPECIAL DIRECTIONS

1. Purchase dehydrated fruit from the store.

2. Melt the colored wax completely. Add scent to the wax.

3. Pour the wax into a bowl.

4. Dip a brush into the wax, paint the wax on the fruit and quickly press it on the candle. Add more wax if needed for adherence. Repeat for each fruit slice.

5. Heat up the remaining wax.

6. Pour wax over the fruit and around the entire candle for better fruit adhesion.

7. Allow the candle to set for 2 hours.

• • •

I'm using an orange wax and orange scent, but you can use any colored wax, dehydrated fruit or scent you'd like. The addition of fruit on a candle provides a look that is festive and fun. These candles look particularly attractive in a living room, dining room or kitchen. The fruit can also be tied to seasons by using apples in the fall or oranges in the summer.

You can substitute cinnamon sticks for small tree branches. I'm using a white candle with a vanilla scent. This candle is handsome, wholesome and rustic-looking. It also makes a beautiful gift.

# Cinnamon Stick Poured Wax Candle

store cost: $15 to $30

handmade cost: $4 to $6

time: 3 hours

SPECIAL TOOLS
*1 old bowl*
*1 small paintbrush or makeup brush*

SPECIAL INGREDIENTS
*8 to 10 ounces wax in the same color as the candle*
*4 to 5 shavings vanilla concentrated candle scent block, or 5 to 6 drops vanilla essential oil*
*cinnamon sticks to cover the candle*
*1 basic poured wax candle*

SPECIAL DIRECTIONS
1. Melt the colored wax completely.

2. Add scent to the wax.

3. Pour the wax into a bowl.

4. Dip a brush into the wax, paint wax on a cinnamon stick and quickly press the cinnamon stick on the candle. Add more wax if needed for adherence. Repeat for each stick.

5. Reheat the remaining wax to 160°F; pour over entire candle.

6. Allow the candle to set for 2 hours.

I'm using red wax with a rose scent. This is a romantic candle, perfect for a beautiful, intimate dinner with someone special. It is also a wonderful candle to light for meditation and contemplation.

# Rosebud Poured Wax Candle

store cost: $15 to $30

handmade cost: $5 to $6

time: 3 hours

SPECIAL TOOLS
*1 old bowl*
*1 small paintbrush or makeup brush*

SPECIAL INGREDIENTS
*8 to 10 ounces wax in the same color as the candle*
*4 to 5 shavings rose concentrated candle scent block, or 5 to 6 drops rose essential oil*
*small rosebuds to cover the candle*
*1 basic poured wax candle*

1. Melt the colored wax completely.

2. Add scent to the wax.

3. Pour the wax into a bowl.

4. Dip a brush into the wax, paint wax on each rosebud and quickly press the rosebud on the candle. Add more wax if needed for adherence.

5. Repeat for each rose.

6. After 1 hour reheat remaining wax to 160°F and pour it over the entire candle.

7. Allow the candle to set for 2 hours.

## Carved Poured Wax Candle

store cost: $15 to $30

handmade cost: $3 to $5

time: 30 minutes to 1 hour

SPECIAL INGREDIENT

*1 basic poured wax candle*

SIMPLE CARVING TECHNIQUES

*Top to bottom straight lines:* Lightly slice the candle from top to bottom in a continuous strip. You can repeat this over the entire candle or alternate with a slice, skip a space, slice, skip a space, etc. This will create a nice contrast between a glossy and matte finish.

*Deep and thin lines:* Use the knife to cut a deep line from top to bottom around the outside of the candle. Next to the line you've just cut, carve another shallow line from top to bottom. Repeat around the candle.

*Circumference lines:* Use the knife to cut a straight line around the entire circumference of the candle. Alternate with a slice, skip a space, slice, skip a space, etc.

*Small circles:* Use the tip of the knife to cut small circles into the surface of the candle. You can do this over the entire candle or in select spaces.

These are just a few suggestions. Be creative and have fun!

. . .

These candles provide a solution to an age-old candle-making problem: how to cover mistakes? I say—carve! Let's say you've poured a candle and remnants of wax from previous candles are left in the mold and cause marring on a new candle. By carving a design along the outside of the candle, you can cover a multitude of imperfections.

# Rolled Beeswax Candles

Rolled beeswax candles impart a beautiful, sweet scent when lit. They are simple to make—all you have to do is roll the wax around a wick, and within a minute or so, you have a finished candle!

Rolled beeswax candles will not burn as long as a poured candle, but are among the easiest, most imaginative and romantic candles you can make.

For rolled beeswax candles, use bleached wicking. This wicking does not have a metal core. Use small bleached wicking for rolled beeswax candles up to 2 inches across. Use medium bleached wicking for candles 2 inches to 3 inches across. Use large bleached wicking for candles 3 inches to 4 inches across.

NOTE: The trick to making a great beeswax candle is to tightly roll the wax sheet around the wick and then to roll the rest of the sheet snugly. The tighter the roll, the longer the candle will burn.

ANOTHER SUGGESTION: When it comes to scenting a beeswax candle, you may prefer not to use a scent. The natural honey fragrance that comes from the beeswax when lit may be all you desire. If you do prefer a scent, here are a few ideas.

• Soak the entire length of the wick in 100% pure essential oil and then wrap the wax sheet around the wick. Let the wick dry for 1 to 2 hours before lighting.

• After the candle is rolled, use an eyedropper and dab 100% pure essential oil down the length of the candle and allow to dry for 1 hour.

• To easily infuse the wick with essential oil, pour the liquid into the bottle's cap. Coil the wick in the cap until the oil is absorbed. Hang the wick over the kitchen faucet to dry. After 1 to 2 hours, wrap the wick in the candle.

# Thick Rolled Beeswax Candle (8-inch)

store cost: $15 to $25

handmade cost: $2.50 to $3.50

time: 10 to 15 minutes

SPECIAL TOOLS

*1 hairdryer*

SPECIAL INGREDIENTS

*1 (8-inch x 17-inch) blue beeswax sheet*
*9 inches small bleached wick*
*5 to 8 drops lavender 100% pure essential oil*

SPECIAL DIRECTIONS

1. Place the beeswax sheet on a cutting board.

2. Optional: Scent the wick with oil.

3. Lay the wick across the 8-inch edge of the sheet.

4. Let 1/2 inch of the wick hang over each end of the sheet.

5. Gently press the wick into the wax.

6. Carefully fold the edge of the sheet over the length of the wick. If the wax starts to break, warm the wax with a hairdryer set on low, until it bends more easily. This should take a few seconds. Do not overheat. You don't want the wax soft, just more malleable.

7. Continue to roll the remainder of the sheet around the wick. Do so evenly, allowing for a snug roll.

8. Snip off 1/2 inch of wick at the bottom and 1/4 inch at the top so only 1/4 inch at the top remains for lighting.

9. Optional: For added scent, drizzle essential oil on the outside of the candle and dry for 1 hour.

. . .

This is a large, elegant candle that can set a mood and burn for awhile. Beautiful alone, or paired with a second candle, the rejuvenating lavender scent complements the blue color of the wax.

# Thin Rolled Beeswax Candle (8-inch)

store cost: $8 to $15

handmade cost: $1.25 to $1.75

time: 10 to 15 minutes

SPECIAL TOOLS

*1 hairdryer*

. . .

By cutting the wax in half, you get two candles from one sheet. While each candle will only burn half as long as the *Thick Rolled Candle*, the look is more conventional and the candle will fit into many traditional candleholders.

*1 (8-inch x 17-inch) orange beeswax sheet*
*9 inches small bleached wick*
*5 to 8 drops tangerine 100% pure essential oil*

SPECIAL DIRECTIONS

1. Place the beeswax sheet on a cutting board.

2. Optional: Scent the wick with oil.

3. With a knife, cut the beeswax sheet in half across the 8-inch middle, or you can fold the sheet in half and bend it back and forth until it tears evenly.

4. Gently press the wick into the wax on the 8-inch edge of the sheet.

5. Let ½ inch of the wick hang over each end.

6. Carefully fold the edge of the wax sheet over the length of the wick.

7. If the wax breaks, warm with a hairdryer set on low, until it bends more easily. Do not overheat.

8. Continue to roll the remainder of the wax sheet around the wick. Do so evenly, allowing for a snug roll.

9. Snip off extra wick at the bottom and ¼ inch at the top for lighting.

10. Optional: Scent the outside of the wax when the candle is completely rolled and dry for 1 hour.

## Thick Rolled Beeswax Candle (4-inch)

store cost: $6 to $12

handmade cost: $1.25 to $1.75

time: 10 to 15 minutes

SPECIAL TOOLS

*1 hairdryer*

SPECIAL INGREDIENTS

*1 (8-inch x 17-inch) purple beeswax sheet*
*5 inches small bleached wick*
*5 to 8 drops 100% pure lavender essential oil*

· · ·

These candles have a warm, French country look. Two candles can be made from a single sheet.

1. Place the beeswax sheet on a cutting board.

2. Optional: Scent the wick with oil.

3. With a knife, cut the beeswax sheet in half across the 17-inch middle, or you can fold the sheet in half and bend back and forth until it separates.

4. Lay the wick across a 4-inch edge of the sheet.

5. Let $1/2$ inch of the wick hang over each end.

6. Carefully fold the edge of the sheet over the length of the wick. If it breaks, warm with a hairdryer set on low, until it bends. Heat for a few seconds only and do not overheat.

7. Continue to snugly and evenly roll the remainder of the sheet around the wick.

8. Cut off $1/2$ inch of the wick at the bottom and $1/4$ inch at the top so $1/4$ inch remains at the top.

9. Optional: Scent the outside of the wax when the candle is fully rolled, and dry for 1 hour.

## Thin Rolled Beeswax Candle (4-inch)

store cost: $5 to $12

handmade cost: Under $1!

time: 10 to 15 minutes

SPECIAL TOOLS

*1 hairdryer*

SPECIAL INGREDIENTS

*1 (8-inch x 17-inch) blue beeswax sheet*
*5 inches small bleached wick*
*5 to 8 drops lemon essential oil*

SPECIAL DIRECTIONS

1. Place the beeswax sheet on a cutting board.

2. Optional: Scent the wick with oil.

3. Cut the beeswax sheet down the middle of the 17-inch side, and then cut down the middle of the 8-inch side. Fold back and forth to loosen until you have 4 equal pieces.

4. Take one of the sheets and lay the wick across a 4-inch edge. Let $1/2$ inch hang over each end. Gently press the wick into the wax.

• • •

Even more economical, one sheet will result in 4 (4-inch rolled) candles!

5. Carefully fold the edge of the sheet over the length of the wick. Use a hairdryer to warm the wax if it starts to break. Continue to snugly fold the remainder of the sheet.

6. Snip off the wick at the bottom and ¼ inch at the top for lighting.

7. Repeat steps 1 through 6 for remaining 3 sheets.

8. Optional: Scent the outside of the wax when the candle is completely rolled and dry for 1 hour.

· · ·

This is a candle with a twist, literally! Dramatic and extremely easy to make, 1 sheet makes 2 candles.

## Diagonal Rolled Beeswax Candle (8-inch)

store cost: $12 to $20

handmade cost: $1.25 to $1.75

time: 10 to 15 minutes

### SPECIAL TOOLS
*1 hairdryer*

### SPECIAL INGREDIENTS
*1 (8-inch x 17-inch) purple beeswax sheet*
*18 inches small bleached wick*
*5 to 8 drops ylang-ylang essential oil*

### SPECIAL DIRECTIONS
1. Place the beeswax sheet on a cutting board.

2. Optional: Scent the wick with oil.

3. With a paring knife, cut the wax diagonally across the 17-inch side.

4. Place the wick across the 17-inch side of 1 of the wax sheets.

5. Let ½ inch of the wick hang over both ends of the sheet.

6. Press the wick into the wax.

7. Carefully fold the edge of the sheet over the length of the wick. Use a hairdryer to warm the wax if it is too stiff.

8. Carefully and securely roll the remainder of the candle.

9. Snip ½ inch of the wick on the bottom and ½ inch on the top.

10. Optional: Scent the outside of the wax when the candle is completely rolled and dry for 1 hour.

# Diagonal Rolled Beeswax Candle (4-inch)

store cost: $8 to $15

handmade cost: Under $1!

time: 10 to 15 minutes

SPECIAL TOOLS

*1 hairdryer*

SPECIAL INGREDIENTS

*1 (8-inch x 17-inch) orange beeswax sheet*
*9 inches small bleached wick*
*5 to 8 drops peach essential oil*

SPECIAL DIRECTIONS

1. Place the beeswax sheet on a cutting board.

2. Optional: Scent the wick with oil.

3. Bend or with a paring knife, cut the wax down the middle of the 8-inch side.

4. Bend or, with a paring knife, cut 1 of the 8-inch pieces at a diagonal down the middle.

5. On 1 of the sheets, lay the wick across the long, diagonal side.

6. Let ½ inch of the wick hang over both ends of the sheet.

7. Press the wick into the wax.

8. Fold the edge of the sheet over the length of wick. Use a hairdryer to warm it if the wax is stiff.

9. Snugly roll the remainder of the wax sheet around the wick.

10. Optional: Scent the outside of the wax and dry for 1 hour.

. . .

This is a very economical candle. A single sheet makes 4 candles.

✳ Notes and Recipes

_____

_____

_____

_____

_____

_____ ＊ ＊ ＊ _____

_____

_____

_____

_____

_____

_____

_____

_____

_____

_____

_____

_____

_____

_____

_____

_____

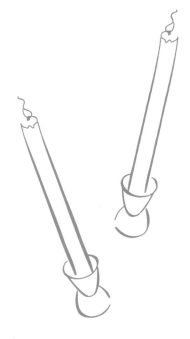

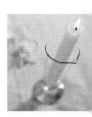

---

---

---

---

---

---

---

---

---

---

---

---

———— ✳ ✳ ✳ ————

---

---

---

---

---

---

---

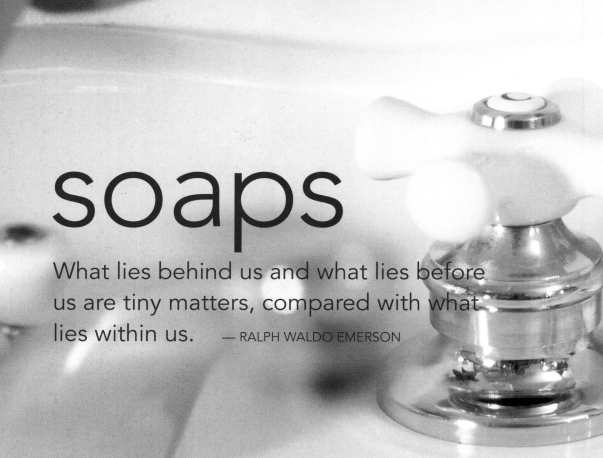

# soaps

What lies behind us and what lies before us are tiny matters, compared with what lies within us. — RALPH WALDO EMERSON

I have long been disappointed with the soap I buy at my local grocery store. It is a transparent bar of soap that usually is "scented," and I use the word scented lightly. It costs about $1.25, tends to be very drying and only lasts a couple of weeks. The one good thing about it is that it's always available.

I've also purchased beautiful handmade soaps for $7 a bar—that's right—$7! They are so beautiful and pricey that I don't want to use them.

So I began searching for a bar that was good, long-lasting, lathered well and looked great, too. Oh, and I didn't want to have to pay a lot per bar. As I was also on a quest to find things to do that were creative and useful, I decided I would add soap-making to the list. Serendipitously I ran into a man selling handmade soaps at a fair. I told him I was interested in making soap, too. He said he taught himself to make soap and it was a lot of fun. He was right.

Creating soap, once you have the timing down, is not as complicated as it might first appear. After you make a few batches, it's rather easy. Like all crafts, the more you do it the easier it becomes. When I made my first batch of soap, I must admit I was nervous, but the bars came out fine and yours will too!

# what is soap?

There are various kinds of soap, such as hard-milled, which involves grating a bar of soap, adding water and other ingredients and re-melting it. The bars tend to be very hard and long-lasting, but not as fresh as with the cold-processed soap method. Commercial soaps are what you buy in the grocery store and are often filled with preservatives, deodorants and other 'itchy' ingredients. Many commercial soap manufacturers remove glycerin, which is unfortunate because glycerin is a wonderful moisturizer.

In this chapter you will learn how to make cold-processed soaps with glycerin. Cold-processed soaps are one of the best soaps available because they are the purest. We will combine oils, such as vegetable oil, with sodium hydroxide (lye) and water to create a chemical reaction, called *saponification*. Saponification is what occurs when the liquids combine and become soap.

### To lard or not to lard

Some soaps have lard in them, but I choose to use vegetable oils instead. I find they work just as well, are cleaner to work with and contain no animal by-products.

### Essential oils

Scent is always added at *trace* (see side note) because essential oils can cause the soap to begin setting up and hardening too quickly. For best results always use 100% pure essential oils, rather than fragrant oils or perfumes that contain alcohol and can impact the soap mixture. Essential oils, while not preservatives per se, do have properties that help extend the life of a bar of soap.

### Natural colors

Oils and fats add their own color to soap and are often creamy yellow and soft white, depending on the tint of the oil. Essential oils will also add some color to a bar of soap. If you are after a distinctive color, here are some ideas: honey can add a golden glow to a bar of soap; green clay adds a blue-gray-green tint; and nori, sushi seaweed wrap, will add a green tint. Cut nori into small strips and place it in a grinder to create a fine powder.

### Cooking temperatures

When heating the oils and fats on a stovetop, I like to use 90°F as my desired temperature. You can go up to 95°F, but do not go below 90°F for best results. These temperatures also work best for the lye solution, which is not heated on the stove, but heats up automatically when it is mixed with water.

### Soap life

The life of cold-processed bar soap is approximately 6 months to 1 year. During that time, you may store soap in a sealed plastic bag in the freezer, or keep it in plastic bags until you're ready to use it. If you leave soap exposed to the air it will still be okay, but it is best to seal it in a bag when the weather is hot or humid.

---

## HELPFUL TERMS

*saponification:* the chemical reaction that produces soap.

*superfat:* a soap with extra oils and fat. The benefit is a highly moisturizing, skin-softening soap.

*trace:* one of the most important terms in soap making. Trace, or trails, occurs when you're preparing soap in a pot and a thread of soap 'dances' on the surface. This lets you know that the soap mixture is ready to be poured into the mold. Trails are not always easy to see. In fact, I often still have trouble with trails. If you take a spoonful of the mixture and drizzle it back into the pot, and a bit of it stays on the surface before sinking into the mixture, then you have achieved trace, or trails. If not, you need to keep stirring.

### Careful when working with sodium hydroxide

Sodium hydroxide, otherwise known as lye, is one of the main ingredients in soap. The chemical is highly caustic, so it is important that you take proper care when mixing lye. (Please do not start using the lye until you have thoroughly read the following paragraphs.)

Always use goggles and gloves and prepare the soap in a well-ventilated area. Keep the lye in a bowl on a flat, sturdy surface. Mix the chemical slowly and do not directly breathe in the fumes, which can be overwhelming. When pouring lye, do so slowly and with the utmost care. Never use lye with children or pets around. Never leave lye out in an unattended area.

The Red Devil brand of sodium hydroxide (lye) can be purchased at most supermarkets, and is often found in the home cleaner aisle.

### Things to look for

*Water on bars:* The moisture you see on the soap is good and means the bars are breathing.

*White powder on bars:* If you get a lot of white powder, then the lye may not have been fully blended into the mixture. If a large portion of the soap has thick white powder on it, throw away the soap and begin again.

*Cottage cheese appearance:* This occurs when ingredients have been miscalculated, or the mixture has been cooled too quickly, resulting in a solid and liquid curdled effect. Discard the soap and try again.

*Excess oil:* When there is a layer of oil, the ingredients were miscalculated. Throw away the soap and try again.

---

### PROJECT TIP | How to mix sodium hydroxide with water

When lye is mixed with purified or distilled water, the fumes can be strong, so you may need to walk away several times during the process.

HERE IS WHAT I LEARNED TO DO
Slowly pour the water into the sodium hydroxide and stir. Then walk away for about half a minute, stir and repeat until the fumes don't bother you. To lessen the strength of the fumes, be sure to mix in a well-ventilated area.

Mix the granules into the water with a stainless steel spoon or a rubber spatula. Mix slowly and evenly until all the granules are dissolved.

almond oil a skin conditioner.

peanut oil rich in vitamin E and less pricey than olive oil. It makes a less fluffy lather, but the bubbles last longer.

coconut oil a skin softener that creates a very fluffy bubble lather.

macadamia oil a skin softener.

avocado oil high in vitamins E, D and A. Also a good skin moisturizer and good for people with sensitive skin.

cocoa butter from the cocoa bean, the same bean that is used in chocolate. It is a fat and an excellent skin moisturizer.

jojoba oil a skin softener from the seeds of a box shrub.

olive oil an excellent moisturizer and helps keep the skin smooth.

vegetable shortening used as a base in soap and works in combination with other oils to bring out their key properties.

# using oils + fats

# General Materials and Tools

*coconut oil*

*vegetable shortening*

*olive oil*

*sodium hydroxide*

*purified or distilled water*

*essential oil*

*cooking spray*

[ Note: Do not use aluminum, as lye will ruin it. Make sure that the beaters of your handmixer are stainless steel; otherwise lye will damage the beaters. ]

*1 food scale (measuring up to 8 pounds)*

*1 (15-gallon) stainless steel stockpot*

*1 pair latex gloves*

*1 pair eye goggles*

*1 (5-quart) heat-resistant glass bowl*

*2 (32-ounce) Pyrex heat-resistance pour pitchers*

*2 long-handled metal spoons*

*2 thermometers (candy making thermometers with clips work best)*

*newspapers*

*1 handmixer, or wooden or stainless steel spoon*

*soap molds*

*1 container plastic wrap*

*1 (10- to 12-gallon) plastic box or cardboard box lined with a garbage bag*

*1 (5- to 8-gallon) plastic box or a cardboard box lined with a garbage bag*

*1 large acrylic cutting board*

*1 paring knife*

## Basic Body Bars: Main Recipe

Each recipe should produce about 20 (6-ounce) bars. However, you can cut the bars larger or smaller, thicker or thinner, depending on your preference. All recipes are for 7½-pound batches. The ingredients can be purchased at your local supermarket or health food store. To save money, don't buy the most expensive brands.

IMPORTANT NOTE: The following directions are to be used as the main directions for all the soap recipes in this chapter. When warranted, special directions will be included for each recipe. Before beginning a recipe, refer back to these instructions.

store cost: $4 to $7 per bar

handmade cost: $1 per bar

time: About 1 hour, and 3 to 4 weeks for bars to set

## INGREDIENTS

*32 ounces coconut oil*

*32 ounces vegetable shortening*

*16 ounces olive oil*

*12 ounces sodium hydroxide*

*28 ounces purified or distilled water*

*10 teaspoons essential oil*

### MEASURING INGREDIENTS

1. On a scale, weigh and then measure the coconut oil and vegetable shortening, and pour into a stockpot. (Do not heat or place the pot on the stovetop.)

2. Place a lid on the pot and set aside.

3. On a scale, measure and then weigh the olive oil and set aside.

### PREPARING THE LYE MIXTURE

1. Put on latex gloves and goggles—make sure your eyes are completely covered.

2. Pour the lye straight from the can into the heat-resistant glass bowl.

3. Weigh the water and pour it into a pitcher.

4. Slowly pour the pitcher of water into the bowl of lye and stir carefully with a spoon, until all the lye is absorbed into the water. When you think everything is absorbed, test the water by scraping the spoon against the bottom of the bowl to see if any lye rises to the top. If lye rises to the top, then keep stirring. If not, then you are ready for the next step.

5. Place the thermometer in the solution. The temperature will likely read 150° to 200°F.

6. Cool down the solution to a temperature of 90°F by placing the bowl in the sink and filling the basin with cold water until it rises to about the same level as the solution in the bowl. If the bowl isn't heavy, the water could knock the solution over, so be very careful. If the bowl is light, then only fill the sink halfway up to the solution level to be safe. Make sure the bowl is steady in the basin and will not tip over. Keep stirring the solution, as this will cause it to cool more quickly. When the temperature drops to about 125°F, stop stirring.

### MIXING OILS AND FATS

1. On medium heat, place the pot of oils on the stovetop and begin stirring briskly with a spoon. Keep stirring until all of the solid fats become liquid and are dissolved.

2. Once the fats are dissolved, turn off the heat, remove the pot to a cool burner and stir in the olive oil. Place a thermometer in the pot. The temperature will likely be around 150°F.

### GLYCERIN SOAPS

You can also make soap from blocks of glycerin. Glycerin soap is made from oil and glycerin, and can be found in an unscented form in most grocery or health food stores. It mixes well with oils, colorants and fragrances. It's usually sold in large blocks and melts down quickly. It works easily in any type of soap mold. You can create and have ready-to-use soap in just a few hours. For more information about how to purchase and use glycerin soap see the following websites: www.ebarge.com, www.craftpals.org, www.eti-usa.com, and www.essentialessences.com

### BALANCING LYE, OILS AND FAT TEMPERATURES

1. Check the temperature of the lye and water. It should drop considerably. When it gets to about 110°F or below, take the mixture out of the water basin and place it on a secure surface that is protected with newspapers. Be careful; if the lye spills it can burn the surface beneath.

2. Place the pot with the dissolved fats in the sink and fill the basin with cold water. To cool down the solution to a temperature of 90°F, place the pot in the sink and fill the basin with cold water until it rises to approximately the same level as the solution in the pot. Make sure that the pot is steady in the basin and will not tip over. To speed up the cooling process, place ice cubes in the sink and stir briskly to help cool the mixture. When the temperature drops to about 125°F, stop stirring.

3. After a few minutes, stop and check the temperature of the lye.

4. The goal is to get the temperature of the mixture in the pot and the bowl to 90°F. You may have to do a bit of going back and forth between the pot and the bowl, to get the temperatures balanced.

5. Once the desired temperatures are reached, remove the pot from the sink, wipe the water from its bottom and place it on the burner. Do not turn on the burner.

### MIXING LYE, OILS AND FATS

1. In the sink, carefully transfer the lye solution to a heat-resistant pitcher. Remember the lye is caustic and can cause burns and scorch the sink if it's spilled, so be careful. When successfully transferred, place the pitcher on a steady surface near the pot of dissolved fats, but away from the burner.

2. On low, start blending the dissolved fats with a handmixer. If using a spoon, begin stirring with even strokes. Slowly pour the lye into the pot of melted oils. Your goal here is to ensure that all of the lye is evenly blended into the fats.

3. Use your handmixer or stir by hand in a continuous movement. If stirring by hand, start to stir more briskly. This will allow the liquid to thicken. You will notice a change in appearance. The mixture will move from thin and clear to thicker and opaque. Initially, your arms and hands will tire from stirring, so transfer handmixer or spoon from one hand to the other, while always stirring continuously at the same pace. Be sure to stir the bottom and sides of the pot, too.

### LOOKING FOR TRACE

1. After 15 to 20 minutes with a handmixer or 30 minutes to 1 hour by spoon, you should test for trace or trailings. With a spoon or spatula, pour a bit of the mixture onto the surface. If you see a gentle ripple that seems to dance on the surface before it sinks back into the mixture, you have trace. These are called trailings or trace because a trace or a trail of the soap is left at the top for just a moment. It is an important indicator because reaching this stage means the mixture is ready to be poured.

I must warn you that trace or trailings are not always easy to spot. Another way to test for trailings is to dip a spoon into the mixture and dapple the liquid on the surface. If a stream of dots sit at the top of the mixture for just a moment and then sink below, that's trace. Do this several times to ensure you see trace. When first starting out, these are particularly hard to see. However, you don't have to continuously stir. If after 20 minutes by handmixer or 1 hour by spoon, you still do not see trailings or trace, stop stirring and assume it is there. After making a few batches you will become a pro at spotting trace.

### ADDING ESSENTIAL OILS

1. After you see the trace, add the essential oils. Blend the oils into the mixture until they have completely disappeared. This shouldn't take more than 30 seconds.

2. Now you have a basic batch of soap. Before pouring it into a mold, lightly spray the plastic mold with a cooking oil, such as Pam. This will help when removing the soap from the mold. Or, if you are using a cardboard box, make sure that the plastic garbage bag is lined flat against the box.

3. Evenly pour the entire contents of the pot into the soap mold.

### SOAP INSULATION PERIOD

1. Cover the top of the mold with clear plastic wrap and stretch taut on top.

2. Place the lid on the plastic box, or close the top of the cardboard box.

3. Wrap the box in heavy blankets, a sweater and a coat to insulate. What I like to do is place a folded sweater in the bottom of a larger box, place the plastic or cardboard box on top, and cover with blankets and a coat. That makes it easy to hold and carry, as well as very stable. Be sure to check that the sweater is folded evenly and that the mold is sitting flat and even, or your soap will set at an angle.

4. Place the box in a cool, dark place, such as a closet or the garage. Do not place the mold in humid areas like the bathroom or kitchen. Leave the mold undisturbed for 24 hours. This will cause a chemical reaction, which heats up the soap and "cooks" the ingredients.

### CURING THE SOAP

1. After 24 hours on a flat and stable surface, remove the insulation, the mold or the box from the larger box and lift the top or lid. Put on your gloves, as the lye is still apparent in the soap. Pull off the plastic wrap.

### REMOVING THE SOAP FROM THE MOLD

1. Touch the soap. It should be somewhat firm with some give. If the soap appears watery or not very firm, re-wrap and re-insulate the bar, and allow it to sit for another 24 hours.

2. Spread newspapers on the area where you plan to remove the soap from the mold. Make sure that the surface is flat and stable.

3. Place a cutting board on your work surface. Spread the sides of the mold apart to loosen the soap. Tap the mold on the sides and bottom. Turn the mold upside down on the cutting board, continue to tap all around sides and keep spreading the sides apart. It may take a bit of work to loosen the soap from the mold, but it should slide out. If you've placed the soap in a cardboard box, pull sides apart to loosen and use the plastic garbage bag to gently lift the soap out.

### SHORT AIR CURE

1. You now have a giant bar of soap. Place the bar in the middle of the cutting board and store it uncovered in a closet, pantry or garage for another 24 hours.

### CUTTING BARS

1. On a stable and flat surface, use a sharp paring knife to score the top, and divide the soap into 20 bars or to your size preference. You may want chunkier bars, slimmer bars, etc.

2. On the cutting board, stand the bars on their sides.

3. Place the uncovered bars back in closet, pantry or garage and allow to "long-cure" for 3 to 4 weeks.

4. Be sure to turn the bars once or twice a week during the long-cure process so all sides are rotated and exposed to air.

### SOAP TIME

1. After 3 to 4 weeks of drying, you now have some of the best soap on the planet — and best of all — you made it yourself. When you feel the richness of the lather, you will know the difference between handmade and commercial soap.

2. Store soap in plastic bags in the freezer or in a bathroom closet, give others away as gifts to family and friends and enjoy!

## Oatmeal and Honey Body Bar

store cost: $4 to $7 per bar

handmade cost: About $1 per bar

time: Less than 1 hour, and 3 to 4 weeks for bars to set

### SPECIAL TOOL
*food processor*

### SPECIAL INGREDIENTS
*½ cup old-fashioned oatmeal*
*3 tablespoons honey*

• • •

The essence of purity, this all-natural soap is a great skin softener that looks and smells delicious.

1. Using a food processor, mince the old-fashioned oatmeal into a fine powder. Do not use instant oatmeal, as it will clump. Set aside.

2. Begin making the *Basic Body Bar: Main Recipe* on pages 40 to 43.

3. After seeing the trace in your basic soap mixture, microwave the honey for about 15 seconds so it is runny.

4. In a bowl, add a cupful of the soap mixture, oatmeal and honey.

5. Whisk together the mixture until it is smooth.

6. Pour the oatmeal-honey mixture back into the main soap mixture, and blend with a spoon or handmixer until smooth. Pour it into the mold.

7. Follow directions for *Soap Insulation Period* through *Soap Time* on pages 43 and 44.

## Loofah Body Bar

<u>store cost</u>: $4 to $7 per bar

<u>handmade cost</u>: About $1 per bar

<u>time</u>: Less than 1 hour, and 3 to 4 weeks for bars to set

SPECIAL TOOL

*food processor*

SPECIAL INGREDIENTS

*2 ounces of a new loofah pad*

SPECIAL DIRECTIONS

1. Cut the loofah pad into thin slices, and cut the slices into 1- to 2-inch pieces.

2. In a food processor, grind pieces into fine particles. It is all right to have some strands of loofah.

3. Pick through and remove any large or hard pieces. The strands should be somewhat loose. Set aside the loofah.

4. Begin making the *Basic Body Bar: Main Recipe* on pages 40 to 43.

5. After seeing the trace in the soap mixture, remove a cupful of the soap and pour it into a bowl. Add the loofah strands to the bowl.

6. Whisk together until smooth. At first the loofah will clump, but keep whisking until it is completely blended. Pour the mixture back into the main soap batch.

7. Blend for about 1 to 2 minutes with a spoon or handmixer, until loofah is completely integrated and smooth. Pour the mixture into a mold.

8. Follow directions for *Soap Insulation Period* through *Soap Time* on pages 43 and 44.

• • •

This bar is great for helping to soften calluses on feet and thinning thick skin on heels. You can buy a loofah pad in your local grocery or health food store.

By using rich oils like macadamia, avocado, almond and jojoba, you are making a truly premium bar. This soap would cost up to $12 per bar in the store if you could find one!

## Luxury Body Bar

store cost: Up to $15 each

handmade cost: About $2 per bar or split the cost with friends

time: Less than 1 hour, and 3 to 4 weeks for bars to set

INGREDIENTS

*32 ounces coconut oil*
*16 ounces macadamia nut oil*
*16 ounces avocado oil*
*8 ounces almond oil*
*4 ounces jojoba oil*
*4 ounces cocoa butter*
*11 ounces sodium hydroxide*
*25 ounces purified or distilled water*
*1½ ounces essential oil, optional*

SPECIAL DIRECTIONS

1. Note: Using the ingredients for this recipe, follow the directions for the *Basic Body Bar: Main Recipe* on pages 40 to 43. Pour the mixture into the mold.

2. Follow directions for *Soap Insulation Period* through *Soap Time* on pages 43 and 44.

## Heavenly Scent Bars

If you love a well-scented bar of soap, you are going to love the following soaps for their incredible fragrances.

This is a fabulous bath bar. The lemon is refreshing, while the lavender is said to be helpful for relaxation. After your bath, while ensconced in your beloved bed, enjoy a few pages of reading from an interesting book and a comforting cup of tea — then it's off to dreamland.

## Lemon and Lavender Body Bar

store cost: $4 to $7 per bar

handmade cost: About $1 per bar

time: Just over 1 hour, and 3 to 4 weeks for bars to set

SPECIAL INGREDIENTS

*5 teaspoons lemon essential oil*
*5 teaspoons lavender essential oil*

SPECIAL DIRECTIONS

1. After you see the trace in your main soap mixture (see pages 42 and 43), pour in the lemon and lavender essential oils.

2. Stir with a spoon until the essential oils are combined, which should take less than 1 minute. Pour the mixture into the mold.

3. Follow directions for *Soap Insulation Period* through *Soap Time* on pages 43 and 44.

## Peppermint Body Bar

store cost: $4 to $7 per bar

handmade cost: About $1 per bar

time: Just over 1 hour, and 3 to 4 weeks for bars to set

SPECIAL INGREDIENTS
*10 teaspoons peppermint essential oil*

SPECIAL DIRECTIONS

1. Make the *Basic Body Bar: Main Recipe* on pages 40 to 43.

2. After you see the trace in your soap mixture (see pages 42 and 43), pour in the peppermint essential oil.

3. Stir with a spoon for less than 1 minute, until all the essential oil is combined.

4. Pour the mixture into the mold.

5. Follow directions for *Soap Insulation Period* through *Soap Time* on pages 43 and 44.

## Creamsicle Body Bar

store cost: $4 to $7 per bar

handmade cost: About $1 per bar

time: Just over 1 hour, and 3 to 4 weeks for bars to set

SPECIAL INGREDIENTS
*5 teaspoons orange essential oil*
*5 teaspoons vanilla essential oil*

SPECIAL DIRECTIONS

1. Make the *Basic Body Bar: Main Recipe* on pages 40 to 43.

2. After you see the trace in your soap mixture (see pages 42 and 43), pour in the orange and vanilla essential oils.

3. Stir with a spoon until all oils are combined, which should take less than 1 minute.

4. Pour the mixture into the mold.

5. Follow directions for *Soap Insulation Period* through *Soap Time* on pages 43 and 44.

• • •

The bracing peppermint makes this soap a great morning wake-up call.

• • •

This is a fun bar of soap that smells like the real thing, bringing back delightful memories of childhood.

## Specialty Soaps

Once you feel confident making soap, it's a lot of fun to make specialty soaps that are as great to look at as they are to wash with!

• • •

This is a beautiful bar of soap that is reminiscent of stained glass and the *Chunk Poured Wax Candle* in the candle-making chapter. It's fun to match the scent with one of the colors of soap you will be using as chunks.

• • •

This soap is akin to *Cathedral Soap*, only the shapes are much smaller. The effect can be subtle, if you use fewer pieces, or strong, if you use a lot. This one reminds me of the *Confetti Poured Wax Candle*. This soap is most attractive when lots of multi-colored soap is used. This is also a great recipe for recycling soap scraps.

## Cathedral Soap

store cost: $5 to $8 per bar

handmade cost: About $1.25 to $1.50 per bar

time: Just over 1 hour, and 3 to 4 weeks for bars to set

### SPECIAL INGREDIENTS

*3 to 4 bars multi-colored transparent and opaque soaps*
*10 teaspoons essential oil of your choice*

### SPECIAL DIRECTIONS

1. Gather your colored bars of soap. The more colors, the better.

2. On a cutting board, use a paring knife to cut triangles, circles, rectangles and squares that are at least 1 inch wide or long.

3. If you want different colors in your bars, cut up a lot of soap pieces, or for less color, cut fewer pieces. The key is to use a good mix of colors.

4. Make *Basic Body Bars: Main Recipe* on pages 40 to 44.

5. After you see the trace, add essential oil.

6. Add the soap chunks to your main soap mixture and stir well for about 1 to 2 minutes.

7. Pour the mixture into the mold.

8. Follow directions for *Soap Insulation Period* through *Soap Time* on pages 43 and 44.

## Confetti Soap

store cost: $4 to $7 per bar

handmade cost: About $1 per bar

time: Just over 1 hour, and 3 to 4 weeks for bars to set

### SPECIAL INGREDIENTS

*1 to 3 bars multi-colored transparent and opaque soaps*
*10 teaspoons essential oil of your choice*

1. To create soap shapes, gather soap bars and scraps of different colors.

2. On a cutting board, use a paring knife to cut very small ¼-inch to ½-inch shreds, slivers and cubes.

3. If you want visual variety in your bars, cut more pieces, or for less diversity use fewer scraps.

4. Make *Basic Body Bars: Main Recipe* on pages 40 to 43.

5. If adding essential oil, add it to the main soap mixture after you see the trace.

6. Use a spoon and stir the soap shapes into the main soap mixture.

7. Pour the mixture into the mold.

8. Follow directions for *Soap Insulation Period* through *Soap Time* on pages 43 and 44.

## Marbled Soap

store cost: $4 to $7 per bar

handmade cost: About $1 a bar

time: Just over 1 hour, and 3 to 4 weeks for bars to set

SPECIAL INGREDIENTS

1½ tablespoons finely ground cinnamon

SPECIAL DIRECTIONS

1. Make *Basic Body Bars: Main Recipe* on pages 40 to 43.

2. After seeing trace in your main soap mixture, remove 30 ounces of the mixture and place in a separate bowl.

3. Into the bowl, add cinnamon.

4. Whisk together for about 1 minute and set aside.

5. Pour the main soap mixture into the mold.

6. Dapple the cinnamon mixture on the main soap mix in the mold.

7. Using the tip of a spatula, draw curlicues and swirls in the mixture. Be sure to create the patterns in the middle and bottom so the cinnamon is distributed throughout.

8. Follow directions for *Soap Insulation Period* through *Soap Time* on pages 43 and 44.

. . .

This soap is incredibly easy to make and will illicit a lot of "oohs and aahs" from family and friends. If you've ever made a marble cake, this will be — well — a piece of cake!

## Basic Facial Bars

Before I started using this recipe, I would spend nearly $30 a month on name-brand cleansers. These facial soaps work so well that I no longer buy expensive facial cleansers.

<u>store cost</u>: $4 to $7 per bar

<u>handmade cost</u>: About $1 a bar

<u>time</u>: Just over 1 hour, and 3 to 4 weeks to set bars

### INGREDIENTS

*32 ounces coconut oil*
*16 ounces almond oil*
*16 ounces vegetable shortening*
*16 ounces peanut oil*
*11 ounces sodium hydroxide*
*25 ounces purified or distilled water*
*1½ ounces essential oil, optional*

### SPECIAL DIRECTIONS

1. Make *Basic Body Bars: Main Recipe* on pages 40 to 43. Pour the mixture into the mold.

2. Follow directions for *Soap Insulation Period* through *Soap Time* on pages 43 and 44.

## Aloe Vera Facial Bar

<u>store cost</u>: $4 to $7 per bar

<u>handmade cost</u>: About $1 a bar

<u>time</u>: Just over 1 hour, and 3 to 4 weeks to set bars

### SPECIAL INGREDIENTS

*3 tablespoons pure aloe vera, gel or liquid*
*1½ ounces essential oil, optional*

### SPECIAL DIRECTIONS

1. Make *Basic Body Bars: Main Recipe* on pages 40 to 43.

2. After you see the trace in your main soap mixture, add aloe vera. Since the aloe vera is already in liquid form, you do not need to make a paste first. With a spoon, stir the mixture well for about 30 seconds. Pour it into the mold.

3. Follow directions for *Soap Insulation Period* through *Soap Time* on pages 43 and 44.

# Aloe Vera and Vitamin E Facial Bar

<u>store cost</u>: $4 to $7 per bar

<u>handmade cost</u>: About $1.25 a bar

<u>time</u>: Just over 1 hour, and 3 to 4 weeks to set bars

SPECIAL INGREDIENTS

*2 tablespoons pure aloe vera, gel or liquid*
*1 tablespoon vitamin E*
*1 1/2 ounces essential oil, optional*

SPECIAL DIRECTIONS

1. Make *Basic Body Bars: Main Recipe* on pages 40 to 43.

2. After you see the trace in the main soap mixture, add aloe vera. Since the aloe vera is already in liquid form, you do not need to make a paste first. With a spoon, stir the mixture well for about 30 seconds.

3. Add vitamin E and essential oil, and stir well for about 30 seconds.

4. Pour the mixture into the mold.

5. Follow directions for *Soap Insulation Period* through *Soap Time* on pages 43 and 44.

# Aloe Vera, Jojoba and Vitamin E Facial Bar

<u>store cost</u>: $4 to $7 per bar

<u>handmade cost</u>: About $1.25 to $1.50 per bar

<u>time</u>: Just over 1 hour, and 3 to 4 weeks to set bars

SPECIAL INGREDIENTS

*2 tablespoons pure aloe vera, gel or liquid*
*1 tablespoon vitamin E*
*1 1/2 ounces essential oil, optional*

SPECIAL DIRECTIONS

1. Make *Basic Body Bars: Main Recipe* on pages 40 to 43.

2. After you see the trace in the main soap recipe, add aloe vera. Since the aloe vera is already in liquid form, you do not need to make a paste first. With a spoon, stir the mixture for about 30 seconds.

3. Add jojoba, vitamin E and essential oil and stir for about 1 minute.

4. Pour the mixture into the mold.

5. Follow directions for *Soap Insulation Period* through *Soap Time* on pages 43 and 44.

This makes a wonderful facial cleanser, but did you know jojoba is also great for hair? It's true. Jojoba is believed by some to promote hair growth on the scalp. For those with thinning hair, give it a try.

## Jojoba Facial Bar

store cost: $4 to $7 per bar

handmade cost: About $1 per bar

time: Just over 1 hour, and 3 to 4 weeks to set bars

SPECIAL INGREDIENTS

*3 tablespoons jojoba oil*
*1¹/₂ ounces essential oil, optional*

SPECIAL DIRECTIONS

1. Make *Basic Body Bars: Main Recipe* on pages 40 to 43.

2. After you see the trace in the main soap recipe, add jojoba. You do not need to make a paste first with the jojoba. With a spoon, stir the mixture well for about 30 seconds.

3. Pour the mixture into the mold.

4. Follow directions for *Soap Insulation Period* through *Soap Time* on pages 43 and 44.

This is a nice skin-smoothing bar and it smells like chocolate.

## Cocoa Butter Facial Bar

store cost: $4 to $7 per bar

handmade cost: About $1 per bar

time: Just over 1 hour, and 3 to 4 weeks to set bars

SPECIAL INGREDIENTS

*3 tablespoons cocoa butter*
*1¹/₂ ounces essential oil, optional*

SPECIAL DIRECTIONS

1. Make *Basic Body Bars: Main Recipe* on pages 40 to 43.

2. After you find trace in your main soap mixture, melt cocoa butter in the microwave for 30 seconds to 1 minute, or until completely melted.

3. Add melted cocoa butter to the main soap mixture. With a spoon, stir the mixture for about 30 seconds.

4. Pour the mixture into the mold.

5. Follow directions for *Soap Insulation Period* through *Soap Time* on pages 43 and 44.

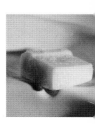

# Cocoa Butter, Jojoba and Vitamin E Facial Bar

store cost: $4 to $7 per bar

handmade cost: About $1.25 to $1.50 per bar

time: Just over 1 hour, and 3 to 4 weeks to set bars

SPECIAL INGREDIENTS

*1 tablespoons cocoa butter*
*1 tablespoon jojoba oil*
*1 tablespoon vitamin E*
*1¹/₂ ounces essential oil, optional*

SPECIAL DIRECTIONS

1. Make *Basic Body Bars: Main Recipe* on pages 40 to 43.

2. After you find the trace in your soap mixture, melt cocoa butter in the microwave for 30 seconds to 1 minute, or until completely melted.

3. Add melted cocoa butter directly to the main soap mixture. With a spoon, stir the mixture well for about 30 seconds.

4. Add jojoba oil, vitamin E and essential oil and stir well for about 30 seconds to 1 minute.

5. Pour the mixture into the mold.

6. Follow directions for *Soap Insulation Period* through *Soap Time* on pages 43 and 44.

# Vitamin E Facial Bar

store cost: $4 to $7 per bar

handmade cost: About $1 per bar

time: Just over 1 hour, and 3 to 4 weeks to set bars

SPECIAL INGREDIENTS

*3 tablespoons vitamin E*
*1¹/₂ ounces essential oil, optional*

SPECIAL DIRECTIONS

1. Make *Basic Body Bars: Main Recipe* on pages 40 to 43.

2. After you see the trace in your soap mixture, add vitamin E and stir well for about 30 seconds.

3. Add essential oil and stir well for about 30 seconds.

4. Pour the mixture into the mold.

5. Follow directions for *Soap Insulation Period* through *Soap Time* on pages 43 and 44.

# Vitamin E and Honey Facial Bar

store cost: $4 to $7 per bar

handmade cost: About $1 per bar

time: Just over 1 hour, and 3 to 4 weeks to set bars

SPECIAL INGREDIENTS
*1¹⁄₂ tablespoons vitamin E*
*1¹⁄₂ tablespoons honey*
*1¹⁄₂ ounces essential oil, optional*

SPECIAL DIRECTIONS

1. Make *Basic Body Bars: Main Recipe* on pages 40 to 43.

2. After you see the trace in your main soap mixture, add vitamin E and stir well for about 30 seconds.

3. Microwave honey for about 15 seconds or until it is runny.

4. Remove 30 ounces of main soap mixture and pour it into a separate bowl.

5. Add honey and whisk together until well mixed.

6. Add honey mixture back into main soap recipe and mix well.

7. Add essential oil and mix well.

8. Pour the mixture into the mold.

9. Follow directions for *Soap Insulation Period* through *Soap Time* on pages 43 and 44.

# French Green Clay Facial Bar

store cost: $4 to $7 per bar

handmade cost: About $1 per bar

time: Just over 1 hour, and 3 to 4 weeks to set bars

SPECIAL INGREDIENTS
*4 ounces French green clay*
*1¹⁄₂ ounces essential oil, optional*

SPECIAL DIRECTIONS

1. Make *Basic Body Bars: Main Recipe* on pages 40 to 43.

2. After you find trace in the main soap mixture, remove 20 ounces and place it in a separate bowl.

• • •

Green clay is often combined with water to form a paste and is used as a mask to tighten the skin. Use once a week to help rejuvenate the skin. Green clay can be found at health food stores.

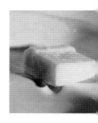

3. Add clay and whisk together until well mixed (this will prevent clumping).

4. Return clay mixture to the main soap recipe and stir well.

5. Mix in essential oil.

6. Pour the mixture into the mold.

7. Follow directions for *Soap Insulation Period* through *Soap Time* on pages 43 and 44.

## Castile Facial Bar

store cost: $4 to $7 per bar

handmade cost: About $1 a bar

time: Just over 1 hour, and 3 to 4 weeks to set bars

SPECIAL INGREDIENTS

*48 ounces olive oil*
*32 ounces coconut oil*
*11 ounces sodium hydroxide*
*26 ounces purified water*
*10 teaspoons orange essential oil*

SPECIAL DIRECTIONS

1. Follow the directions for *Basic Body Bars: Main Recipe* on pages 40 to 43. Substitute the ingredients from the main recipe with the special ingredients listed here.

2. Pour the mixture into the mold.

3. Follow directions for *Soap Insulation Period* through *Soap Time* on pages 43 and 44.

• • •

This is my favorite soap, it is so pure and clean. I alternate it with the *Basic Facial Bar* and variations of it, but I always use a bar of castile soap every other day. Used in Europe for centuries, this soap helps make skin smooth and clean. There are no suggested variations for this soap since it is perfect.

# ✳ Notes and Recipes

_____

_____

_____

_____

_____

_____ * * * _____

_____

_____

_____

_____

_____

_____

_____

_____

_____

_____

_____

_____

_____

_____

* * *

* * *

# essential potpourri

The present moment is a powerful goddess.

— GOETHE

How often have you gone into someone's home and immediately experienced a wonderful calming scent? Your eyes glance to the source and you find a bowl of colorful potpourri. You buy some at a local store. But after a short time the scent fades, or the colors are not exactly what you wanted. You may also find wood in your pricey potpourri, which is used as an inexpensive filler in the overall mix. You realize that the potpourri, while nice, was never exactly what you wanted. You only bought it because there wasn't much variety to choose from.

The wonderful thing about creating *Calming Craft* potpourri is that you get to customize, and create exactly what you want. With more than 100 kinds of dried botanicals, plants, fruits, flowers, herbs and scents to choose from, your choices are limitless.

The reason I started making potpourri is because I couldn't find potpourri in the exact scent and colors I wanted. How hard could it be to make potpourri? You'll find making potpourri is one of the simplest, most creative and gratifying *Calming Crafts* you can do at home.

## How to dry potpourri

It is easy to dry your own potpourri ingredients. By tying them together with string or a rubber band, you can hang them upside down in a protected area, attaching them to a wall or ceiling. Place a bowl underneath the hanging flowers to catch falling petals. Or, stand the flower bunch upside down in a bowl and set it on a table or counter and the leaves will fall into the vessel. This method works well for flowers and plants.

Place freshly picked flowers and leaves on a clear white paper towel and store them in a cupboard for 2 to 7 days or until they are dry to the touch. Always keep ingredients in an airtight container, preferably glass, or a plastic bag cinched tight, or a paper bag closed and sealed with tape.

You can dry the ingredients yourself or buy them at the grocery store, health food store or through mail order. Many major cities also have stores that sell tea, spices, dried botanicals and flowers. Look in the phone book under spices and tea to see if there is a store near you.

I happened upon a wonderful little store in the colorful and vibrant Mission section of San Francisco and found a cornucopia of potpourri ingredients and scents.

I filled a hand-basket four times with interesting dried flowers, pine cones, herbs and fruits. Some, like arti pods, sounded and looked exotic. An arti pod comes in sections and looks like tree bark in the shape of a pear. Others I had only heard of in reference to tea, like chamomile, but now saw what they looked like whole — dime-sized, off-white colored pompons. Some herbs like lemon verbena were so fragrant that I bought a pound's worth, figuring I would find a way to use it all. I did!

Cones evoked fond remembrances of long, revitalizing hikes in the woods, far away from work, commitments, family and friends — just me, alone in thought. I also bought several bottles of essential oils and fragrances.

Then I got home and started mixing. After lots of experimentation, I came up with recipes that brighten my home, my car, my office and my attitude. I'd like to share these recipes with you so you can enjoy them too.

## Fillers

The ingredients that go into making potpourri are called fillers. These include flowers, plants, herbs, spices, cones, grasses and other botanicals.

## Fixatives

A fixative is like a sponge: it's used to absorb and hold fragrance in potpourri. The following are often used as fixatives: cellulose, orris root, oak moss, calamus root, citrus peels and spices such as cloves.

Cellulose is probably my favorite, because it is odorless and takes on whatever scent you apply to it. Cellulose resembles small pebbles and looks similar to the cereal Grape Nuts. Cellulose is cream in color, blends well with most potpourri and because the pebbles have a bit of weight to them, it tends to sink to the bottom of a potpourri,

which is helpful if you want it for scent and not aesthetics. Cellulose comes from a cob of corn and is extremely porous and inexpensive, averaging about 25 cents per ounce. Oak moss, on the other hand, has a slight outdoorsy scent and look, can really enhance the appearance of certain potpourri and averages about 50 cents per ounce.

## Fragrance

There are basically three different kinds of fragrance: essential oils, fragrance oils and the natural scents from the potpourri fillers.

Essential oils are 100% pure oils derived from the essences of plants, fruits, flowers, herbs and plants. These have the strongest and most long-lasting scents. They are also completely natural. Prices range from around $2 for a 1-ounce bottle of wintergreen scent to about $10 for a 1-ounce bottle of frankincense essential oil.

Fragrance oils are blends of essential oils, synthetic oils and additives in an alcohol base. The disadvantage of fragrance oils is that they are not 100% natural. The advantage is that you have a myriad of scents from which to choose, while with essential oils you are limited to available plants, fruits and botanicals. With fragrance oils you have a choice of natural and synthetic scents and scent combinations such as apple and spice, bayberry, chocolate, rain forest, rose garden, spring floral, tropical, winterberry and even java.

Prices average just under $4 for a 1-ounce bottle of fragrance oil. In some cases, prices are about the same for fragrance oils and essential oils. I priced a bottle of orange scent essential oil at $3.45, while the fragrant oil version was $3.35. However, sometimes the fragrance oil version can be a lot less. I priced frankincense at $10 for the essential oil version, and $3.70 for the fragrance oil.

Natural scents are the fragrances from the blend of flowers, spices, fruits, herbs and plants in potpourri. The scent will probably be subtle. If that is appealing to you, then that may be all you need. However, if you prefer a stronger scent in your potpourri, I suggest using essential oils or fragrance oil. You can even use a combination if you like. Remember that the scents from a fragrance or oil you choose will blend with the natural scents from the potpourri filler to form an overall unique aroma.

## Dry versus wet look

Like hair, potpourri can have a dry or oily look. Classic potpourri has a dry look, meaning the colors, unless dyed, look natural. You can always tell oily potpourri because it has a darker sheen and the filler looks soaked or drenched. The flowers, cones and other ingredients appear darker than normal.

The oily look is achieved by applying fragrance oil or essential oil directly on the ingredients. Some fillers like lemon verbena will turn from a light to a very dark color when oil is applied.

Classic potpourri is dry. Scent is applied to a fixative, which absorbs most of the oil, and the dry ingredients are then tossed with the fixative. The filler picks up scent when it is enclosed in an airtight environment with the fixative.

## sampling of fillers

allspice: dark brown, fragrant berries

angel wings: wispy white flowers often bleached or dyed pink

apple slices

bael nut slices: dark orange interiors and wood-like exteriors

balsam fir needles: resemble grass, but smell like Christmas

cedar tips: green

cockscomb flowers: red with velvet-like clusters and tartly scented

cornflowers

curly pods

eucalyptus leaves: blue-gray

globe amaranth: white, round flowers

juniper berries: red

larkspur petals: blue

lemon verbena leaves: green curled leaves with potent lemon scents

malva flowers: piercing purple-blue

milo berries: pretty cranberry

orange peel slices

pearly everlasting: white sprigs

pine cones, hemlock: small cones in gray-brown

pine cones, ponderosa: nicely scented in brown

pine cones, white spruce: brown and round

pomegranates: red-magenta

repends flowers: red with long blades

rhododendron: green and excellent for color

rosebuds: small tight buds in red, pink and yellow

rose hips: whole peas in deep, pretty magenta

senna pods: nice brown leaves

statice flowers: pretty in yellow, purple and white

strawflowers: yellow, dainty flowers

tilia flowers: dark orange hue

velvet flowers: red or orange

There isn't a wrong way or a right way when it comes to the look of your potpourri. Perhaps you want some potpourri to appear light, while you prefer others to be dark. You might even want to mix the two in a single batch. The choice is yours!

### Quick cure

The longer you cure potpourri, the more everlasting your scent will be. If you don't have 2 to 4 weeks to cure your potpourri, and want to make it in the same day — you can.

If you can cover the potpourri in an airtight container for even a few hours, a little bit of curing is better than no curing at all. But even if you don't have time to cure, you can still instantly make and use potpourri. It just won't last as long as cured potpourri, but it will work in a pinch. The potpourri could last a month or several months. It just depends on the amount of essential oil used and how it interacts with the other ingredients.

I call this the instant potpourri method. Place extra essential oil on the fixative or directly on the potpourri. The key is to use essential oils. Fragrance oils are made with alcohol and dissipate into the air more quickly than pure essential oils. This is not a problem when adequate time is given for curing. However, when pressed for time, essential oils are the way to go because the oils allow scent to quickly adhere to potpourri. An essential oil scent will also last longer than fragrance oils when making instant potpourri.

## Making potpourri

While some of the chapters contain very specific directions, the creation of potpourri is more about art than it is about following directions. You are only limited by your imagination. And like cooking or painting, you can be creative. If you have never thought of yourself as creative, making potpourri will bring out the latent artist in you. It is all about mixing and blending elements, textures, colors and scents to create a unified whole.

When it comes to making potpourri, there are many variables. It is difficult to say how much of an ingredient you might need in a suggested recipe because it *is* only a suggestion. You may want to create a lot of something or just a little. In addition, the difficulty of suggesting amounts for each ingredient depends on the volume and size of the jar or plastic bag you are using. That is why the recipes in this chapter give ingredients, but not amounts. That is up to you.

With potpourri, nothing goes to waste. Whatever does not fit into a potpourri jar can be placed in a bowl or put into muslin bags for sachets. You can have potpourri in every room of your house.

## General Materials and Tools

*fillers*

*fixatives*

*fragrance*

[ Note: Plastic will retain the scent of potpourri, so for stronger scents use nonplastic bowls. ]

*newspapers*

*1 large nonplastic bowl*

*1 small nonplastic bowl*

*2 nonplastic spoons*

*1-quart pitcher*

*glass jars, any size*

## Layered Potpourri

To buy layered potpourri in a store is expensive, but to make it yourself is not. Since the inspiration behind creating potpourri is primarily visual, a clear jar is suggested. Color comes first, followed by ingredients and then scent. You might be inspired by the muted colors of springtime, or potpourri with lots of odd shapes and sharp edges. The colors of your home may spark your artistry. Or perhaps you will find inspiration from your children.

Once you choose the colors, then select the fillers. What works really well in layered potpourri is contrasting textures. You might take a leaf that has a spiral effect, such as curly pods, and add a layering of smooth leaves, like senna pods. You might use pearly everlasting sprigs that have a light, white color with a fluffy texture and place them next to vanilla-infused cellulose, which has a creamy color and a pebble-like texture.

You can decide how you want to layer and pair ingredients together. Break up layers with different ingredients or place similar ingredients on the top of each other. You can put as much or as little of an ingredient in a layer. If you want a tight, even look, then use your hand or a spoon to pack the ingredients. If you like a more spontaneous, natural look, pack the layers more loosely. Continue to place and overlay your ingredients until you reach the top.

When you are done, include a fixative in your mix, or place several drops of fragrance oils or essential oils on the top layer of your potpourri. Place potpourri in a jar with an airtight lid, seal and let it cure for 2 to 4 weeks.

Remember that there is no right or wrong way to make layered potpourri. Let the possibilities of what you can create, what appeals to you and your imagination run wild. Experiment! Have fun! Be creative!

store cost: All natural potpourri, absent of wood and artificial ingredients, could cost as much as $30 for a 3-ounce bag.

handmade cost: About $2 to $10, depending on ingredients, for about 3 ounces. Costs will be less or more depending on ingredients and quantity. Since you decide the amounts, it is difficult to give actual costs.

time: 10 to 15 minutes to blend, and curing time of 2 to 4 weeks

DIRECTIONS

The directions below are suggestions for creating potpourri.

1. Spread newspapers over your work area since oils can stain.

2. On your work area, lay out your bags of filler. You may want to have your tools laid out. Group all the flowers together by color, arrange the fruits and repeat with spices, cones and other ingredients.

3. Line up your bottles of scents.

4. Choose a potpourri theme, either by scent or decorative aesthetics.

5. If your theme is fragrance, choose a fixative. In this example, I've selected a vanilla fragrance and chose cellulose as a fixative (cellulose is cream in color and goes along nicely with a vanilla fragrance).

6. In a bowl, pour a handful of cellulose.

7. Add 4 to 7 drops of vanilla, depending on your desired strength. If you want it really strong, add more vanilla. Use a spoon to blend ingredients.

8. Add fillers that match a vanilla theme, such as flowers that are white and vanilla-colored, light-brown cones, cinnamon sticks or brown leaves.

9. Use a spoon to blend the mixture together. Scoop ingredients into a pitcher.

10. Pour ingredients into a covered jar of your choice.

11. Pack loosely at the top, cover with an airtight lid and shake.

12. Store in a warm, dry place like a cupboard or a closet, and shake the jar every few days.

13. Allow the fixative, filler and fragrance to cure for 2 to 4 weeks.

14. Now you are ready to open the jar of potpourri, or pour it into another bowl for display.

15. The potpourri scent will last from 6 months to 1 year or longer.

16. To refresh, simply add several drops of scent to the mix.

## VARIATIONS ON DIRECTIONS

1. You may decide to become inspired by the filler first and then choose a scent after you've completed most of the potpourri. For example, you may look at the ingredients and envision potpourri resembling a spring day, and see the colors green, purple and yellow. You might take a few handfuls of bright green rhododendron leaves as a base, and add purple malva flowers with bright yellow strawflowers. Then you decide that you want a really fun element that won't overpower the flowers, so you add white pearly everlasting sprigs and so on.

2. Once you have the decorative items you desire, envision the scent. For example, there is a fragrant oil called spring garden that would go nicely with spring-inspired potpourri.

3. Choose a fixative; in this case I picked a handful of oak moss.

4. Place the ingredients in a bowl.

5. Add 6 drops of Spring Garden fragrance.

6. With a spoon, mix for 5 minutes.

7. Transfer the mixture to an airtight jar.

8. Shake it every few days.

9. Store it in a dry, warm place for 2 to 4 weeks.

## The Great Outdoors

theme: nature

hues: browns, whites

scent: vanilla

TOP LAYER
  *curly pods*

MIDDLE LAYER
  *vanilla-infused cellulose*
  *pearly everlasting*

BOTTOM LAYER
  *vanilla-infused cellulose*

## Vanilla Spice

theme: kitchen warmth

hues: white, cream and brown

scent: vanilla and cinnamon

TOP LAYER
  *pearly everlasting*

MIDDLE LAYER
  *cinnamon sticks*

BOTTOM LAYER
  *white globes*

SPRINKLED THROUGHOUT:
*vanilla-infused cellulose*

## Colors

theme: different colored layers

hues: the rainbow

scent: cloves and lemon

TOP LAYER
  *malva flowers, blue*

MIDDLE LAYER
  *tilia flowers, orange*
  *strawflowers, yellow*
  *malva flowers, blue*
  *milo berries, cranberry*

BOTTOM LAYER
  *rhododendron, dark green*

SPRINKLED THROUGHOUT:
*lemon-infused cloves*

## Tropical Paradise

theme: fun, carefree tropics

hues: pinks, yellows and oranges

scent: orange

TOP LAYER
  *strawflowers*

MIDDLE LAYER
  *repens flowers*
  *strawflowers*
  *tilia flowers*
  *orange slices infused with
    orange scent*
  *orange velvet flowers*

BOTTOM LAYER
  *strawflowers*

## Spontaneous Potpourri: Bowl and Jar Mixes

When inspiration strikes, you want to create and you want to do it now! This is known as instant gratification. *Calming Crafts* are a wonderful way to slow down, reflect and enjoy the moment, rather than worrying about the past or thinking about the future.

Since falling in love with making potpourri, I have found a way to bridge my need for spontaneity with the scent blending requirements of potpourri — I plan ahead. I infuse cellulose with scents I like and scents that I know will blend well together. I keep them in airtight mason jars and store them in a kitchen cupboard.

At any time, I will have separate jars of cellulose infused with the essential oils of vanilla, orange, strawberry, lavender, lemon and peppermint. I'll arrange my potpourri ingredients on a table, select a decorative bowl or jar to display the potpourri in and then I start to create.

I find the process to be very much a building one. First I choose a scent and then I pour a scent-infused fixative on the bottom of the bowl or jar so the scent will rise up and blend with the other ingredients. I think about the leaf colors, shapes and how they will look in the bowl. Then I choose flowers based on colors that blend and contrast. I might lighten or darken the overall look with sprigs or cones, while always keeping in mind the shapes of the ingredients. If the botanicals are too angled, I might soften the look with ingredients that will affect the overall presentation of the mix. I'll also sprinkle scent-infused cellulose atop to enhance the fragrance of the entire mix.

Also, when creating spontaneous potpourri, think about the vessel you will display the mix in, since that will influence your design.

This kind of potpourri is great when you need to do something creative, because it provides instant gratification as well as a wonderful gift for you and last-minute gifts for friends or family, too.

## Spring Mix

I knew that I wanted to make potpourri that in its own way reminded me of springtime. It was winter and I was longing for beautiful colors, something beyond the grays and blacks of January. I wanted a look that was colorful. The color purple came to mind and I knew the potpourri had to include the scent of lemon verbena.

In a big bowl, I placed two handfuls of lemon verbena leaves. To satisfy the color I envisioned, I tossed in purple malva flowers. I mixed them both and noticed how well the purple complemented the light-green lemon verbena leaves. But a brighter color was needed, so I added a handful of yellow strawflowers. The contrast between light and dark colors was impressive. Next, I worked on the shapes of the ingredients. The curled edges of the lemon verbena leaves needed something softer and rounder, so I added whole rose hips. The rose hips added a pleasant, cranberry color and a pleasing, spicy scent. But the ingredients, which were all fairly small in size, required something larger, almost a playful element. Then I knew exactly what was required — bael nut

slices. The inside of a bael nut looks a bit like an orange with every drop of moisture removed, resulting in a dark orange hue. Its skin is rough and light brown and resembles tree bark. Just a few tosses and in moments I had the right mix, the perfect blend.

<u>theme</u>: springtime

<u>hues</u>: green, yellow, purple and cranberry

<u>scent</u>: tropical (The fragrant scent of lemon verbena blends well with a tropical scent.)

*lemon verbena*
*bael nut slices*
*rose hips, whole*
*malva flowers, purple*
*strawflowers*
*tropical-infused cellulose*

## Bright Flowers

Sprinkle lavender essential oil directly onto the flowers if you want the flowers to have darker hues. The contrast of light and dark has an intriguing look and is quite attractive.

<u>theme</u>: pretty flowers

<u>hues</u>: yellow, purple, cranberry and orange

<u>scent</u>: lavender

*strawflowers, yellow*
*malva flowers, purple*
*velvet flowers, orange*
*milo berries, cranberry*

## Citrus Dreams

<u>theme</u>: fruit

<u>hues</u>: orange, cranberry, cream, red and magenta

<u>scent</u>: orange and lemon

*orange slices*
*lemon slices*
*apple slices*
*whole rose hips*
*pomegranates*

# Garden Delights

I chose a round, dark-green bowl with circles alternating light-yellow stripes. I poured lemon-infused cellulose on the bottom of the bowl, and on top sprinkled two handfuls of linden flowers for their light green and brown colors. That, to me, was the grass.

Now I had to plant the flowers. I choose sunflower petals because of their muted yellow color, which reminded me of a pretty, hazy spring day. I sprinkled a little more cellulose and then added yarrow sprigs for their dark yellow, brownish color. I also liked the sprig's light, woodsy scent, which blended well with lemon. There was a nice visual contrast between the shorter linden flower leaves and the long, thin yarrow sprigs. A burst of color was needed, so I added milo berries for their intense cranberry color. That was the secret ingredient that made the look I was after. I sprinkled more cellulose on top for scent, and because the cellulose's cream color blended so well with the look of the mix. I set the bowl on a living room table and immediately the room was infused with the pleasing scent of lemon.

theme: the happy, healthy feeling of being in a garden

hues: greens, browns and yellows

scent: lemon

*linden flowers*
*sunflower petals*
*yarrow sprigs*
*milo berry, just a few sprigs for color*

# In the Forest

The day I came up with this mix I was going to go for a hike, but it was raining, so instead I recreated nature in a bowl.

The rhododendron leaves I bought were dyed a deep green. I chose that color as a base to reflect water on the leaves, which would make them darker. I sprinkled a thin layer of the leaves on the bottom of a wide, but shallow clay-colored round dish. One of the things I love best about hiking is the smell of the outdoors. Since I was forced to be indoors on that day, the potpourri gave me the opportunity to remember the heavenly scents.

On top of the leaves, I arranged clumps of oak moss infused with balsam fir and separate clumps of oak moss infused with eucalyptus. The light brown and green color of the oak moss really stood out against the bright green leaves. I tossed in liberal handfuls of hibiscus pods. The light brown and pinks of the open, roundish pods gave a real sense of being outdoors. But a darker color was needed to bring texture to the blend,

so I added a handful of dark-brown, whole hibiscus flowers. I added a few sprigs of oak moss on top, placed the dish on the living room table and watched the rain outside.

<u>theme</u>: walking through the forest

<u>hues</u>: browns, light and dark with a touch of green

<u>scent</u>: balsam fir and eucalyptus

*rhododendron leaves, bright-green dyed*
*oak moss infused with balsam fir essential oil*
*oak moss infused with eucalyptus essential oil*
*hibiscus pods*
*hibiscus flowers, whole*

## Winter Mix

This is another woodsy mix that takes advantage of the dark brown colors of winter. I love the crisp and clean look of the coldest season. There is a minimalist beauty to the outdoors when the leaves have fallen, branches are bare and the naked beauty of the trees remain. To somewhat recreate that feeling and look, I produced a mix that emphasizes the woods and cones, with flowers in the background to add a touch of color and light.

In a cream-colored bowl, I scattered noble fir cone scales, which have a rosy, woody look. Next, I added 2- to-3-inch spruce cones. To complement the dark brown of the spruce, I added handfuls of highly textured arti pods. The pear-shaped pods are unusual in shape, and contrast well with the scaled spruce. To lighten the dark mix, I added cream-colored chamomile pods. To blend the hues together, I added pearly everlasting. On top, I added deep-brown, curlicue tail springs, which are woody vine coils, about 6 inches long. They may be placed as is or cut shorter. I tossed in several long tail springs. The unusual shapes of the arti pods and tail springs gave the mix a nice, earthy, yet artsy look.

<u>theme</u>: the woody look of winter

<u>hues</u>: browns with hint of white

<u>scent</u>: no oil scent, just the scent from the cones and flowers

*noble fir cone scales*
*spruce cones*
*arti pods*
*chamomile*
*tail spring*
*pearly everlasting*

# Lavender and Purple

My idea for this potpourri was to create a relaxing mix for the bathroom, something with a gentle, warming scent that was not too overwhelming. I started with lavender seeds for their lilac color and scent. Since lavender was my theme, I added malva flowers for their deep, purple-blue color and natural complement. I thought about using just these two ingredients in the mix, which would have been fine, but decided I wanted something more colorful.

In a small clear bowl, I added a handful each of lavender seeds and malva flowers. Then for additional color, I tossed in some sprigs of pearly everlasting and a generous toss of strawflowers. The muted yellows of the strawflowers blended beautifully with the lilac and purple of the lavender and malva. Just a few tosses of rhododendron leaves and a more generous handful of lemon verbena for its light green leaves, and the look was almost complete. I added a couple of slices of bael nuts, primarily for their unusual shape and look.

theme: purple

hues: light and dark purple, yellows, greens and whites

scent: lavender seeds, no oils

*lavender seeds*
*malva flowers, purple-blue*
*pearly everlasting*
*strawflowers*
*rhododendron leaves*
*lemon verbena*
*bael nuts*

# Pretty Peppermint

This mix has a strong peppermint scent that can hide and absorb fragrance. Start by lining the bottom of a bowl with cloves infused with peppermint. Then add the rhododendron leaves, followed by both kinds of hibiscus. Add more cloves, followed by apple slices, chamomile flowers and tilia and strawflowers for their orange and yellow colors. Sprinkle a few cloves on top and within minutes you have a beautiful and wonderfully scented mix.

theme: pretty and light

hues: yellows, pinks and cranberries

scent: clove infused with peppermint essential oil

*hibiscus pods*
*hibiscus flowers, whole*
*rhododendron leaves*
*apple slices*
*chamomile*
*tilia flowers*
*cloves infused with peppermint essential oil*

## Romantic Mix

Love is in the air. I added handfuls of fall-colored flowers and cones to give a warm look to this potpourri. The lemon-orange scent enriches the color and reminds me of a crisp autumn day. When it comes to scents, as always, I only offer suggestions, so please choose a scent that you find romantic.

<u>theme</u>: love

<u>hues</u>: yellows and pinks

<u>scent</u>: lemon-orange

*curly pods*
*senna pods*
*white spruce cones*
*repens flower*
*arti pods*
*noble fir scales*
*rose hips, whole*
*pomegranates*
*sunflower petals*
*oak moss infused with lemon-orange*

## Pale Mix

This simple mix is also very romantic, as well as beautiful. Start with a base of cellulose infused with rosewood essential oil. Fill the bowl with primary ingredients of rosebuds, rosebud petals and hibiscus pods. To bring out the pink color, contrast with sunflowers. Add a couple of arti pods for texture, and a few sprigs of milo berries for their deep cranberry color. These colors will blend with the pinks and everything will come up smelling of roses.

<u>theme</u>: pale colors

<u>hues</u>: pinks

<u>scent</u>: rosewood

*rosebuds*
*rosebud petals*
*hibiscus pods*
*sunflowers*
*arti pods*
*milo berries*
*cellulose infused with rosewood essential oil*

## Magenta Mix

The muted hues of magenta and vanilla blend well together so I used both. Hibiscus pods and whole hibiscus was the base, creating a pleasing contrast of light and dark. I added a few curly pods and a small handful of noble fir scales. I strategically dropped pinches of tilia flowers to bring out lighter tones. For color and sense of play, I added dried pomegranates. Then I liberally sprinkled vanilla essential oil over the entire mix. (I couldn't find a fixative I liked with this mix so I poured vanilla essential oil directly onto the ingredients.) About once a month, I add a couple of drops to the mix to keep it fresh.

<u>theme</u>: the color magenta

<u>hues</u>: magenta, pinks and browns

<u>scent</u>: vanilla

*hibiscus pods*
*hibiscus flowers, whole*
*tilia flowers*
*pomegranates*
*curly pods*
*noble fir scales*

## Green is Great!

This mix was an experiment in using primarily leaves and the color green. The mix blends beautifully in rooms with brown and green hues. *Green is Great!* is also fun to make because of its simplicity — grab handfuls of each ingredient and toss them into a bowl or a jar. The mix has various hues of green, from the dark rhododendron to light-green linden flowers, lemon verbena and oak moss. There is also a subtle touch of yellow in the mix from the linden flowers and leaf ingredients.

<u>theme</u>: everything green

<u>hues</u>: green

<u>scent</u>: wintergreen essential oil

*rhododendron leaves*
*linden flowers and leaves*
*lemon verbena*
*oak moss infused with wintergreen*

## Fruit and Flowers

From beautiful fruit to colorful flowers and delicious scents, the wonders of nature can be found in this mix. At the bottom of the bowl, place a good amount of cellulose infused with lemon essential oil. Fill the bowl halfway with strawflowers as the base. Add sprinkles of rhododendron leaves, malva flowers and rose hips for bright color. For some muted tones, place apple slices and additional sprinkles of cellulose. To the top, add a bael nut slice and a couple of pomegranates. Place the potpourri on a table and enjoy it with a soothing cup of raspberry zinger tea.

<u>theme</u>: nature's bounty

<u>hues</u>: bright yellow, purple and cranberry

<u>scent</u>: lemon

*strawflowers*
*malva flowers*
*apple slices*
*orange slices*
*pomegranates*
*bael nuts*
*rose hips, whole*
*cellulose infused with lemon essential oil*

# Potpourri Sachets

A good policy for making potpourri is that nothing should go to waste. In that spirit, potpourri sachets are a terrific way to use extra potpourri ingredients. I make and use them all the time. I keep potpourri sachets in my car, office, purse, pockets of coats, closets and in every room of the house.

Sachets also make exceptionally nice gifts. I use them as thank-you presents. I've given them to my mailman, a favorite checker at the grocery store, my massage therapist, co-workers and my doctor's receptionist, as well as family and friends. They are easy to make and take under a minute to assemble.

The scent will last anywhere from 3 months to 1 year or more. To refreshen, simply squeeze the bag.

Potpourri sachets can have as many or as few ingredients as you like. The key is to use essential oils and preferably a fixative for longer scent hold. The principles of making potpourri apply to sachets.

## TO BEGIN

Muslin bags come in small, medium and large sizes, and can be purchased by mail order (see *Suppliers Resource List* on page 124) or found in some health food stores. If your local health food store does not have them, ask if the bags can be special-ordered.

Fill the sachet bags with leftover potpourri ingredients. I like to fill mine so they are plump. Cinch the bag with a knot to close and that's it!

You can also make potpourri especially for sachets. When I do this, I like to keep the ingredients to a minimum. I usually use a scent-infused fixative and a single ingredient. The fabric of the bag hides sachet potpourri, so the scent is the most important factor. As with displayed potpourri, try to infuse the fixative with a scent ahead of time, say a day to a couple of weeks, and then blend it with an ingredient. If you are in a pinch, the fixative and ingredient can be mixed in a bowl, dried for 1 hour and then placed in a muslin bag.

I've included several recipes that I've had a lot of fun with. These are specifically made for sachet potpourri. Unless otherwise noted, the scent infusion is from essential oils. I usually use cellulose as my fixative, since cellulose holds scents best within muslin bags.

## USE THE FOLLOWING STEPS FOR ALL THE SACHET RECIPES

1. Blend a scent-infused fixative and an ingredient.

2. Fill a muslin bag with ingredients.

3. Tie the bag shut.

## Tropical Scent

*tropic fragrant oil-infused cellulose*
*sunflower petals*

## Vanilla

*vanilla-infused cellulose*
*chamomile flowers*

## Sweet Dreams

*lavender seeds*
*chamomile flowers*

## Lemon and Lavender

*lemon-infused cellulose*
*lavender seeds*
*white globes*

## Vanilla and Lavender

*vanilla-infused cellulose*
*lavender seeds*

## Peppermint and Lavender

*peppermint-infused cellulose*
*lavender seeds*

## Lemon Zest

*lemon-infused cellulose*
*lemon verbena*

## Vanilla Spice

*vanilla-infused cellulose*
*spruce cones*

## Lemon and Orange

*lemon-infused cellulose*
*orange-infused cellulose*
*oak moss*

## Orange Creamsicle

*orange-infused cellulose*
*vanilla-infused cellulose*
*white globes*

## ✳ Notes and Recipes

---

---

---

---

---

————————— ✳ ✳ ✳ —————————

---

---

---

---

---

---

---

---

---

---

---

---

---

\* \* \*

\* \* \*

## ✳ Notes and Recipes

* * *

_____

_____ * * * _____

_____

_____

_____

_____

_____

_____

_____

_____

_____

_____

_____

_____

_____

_____

_____

_____ * * * _____

_____

_____

_____

# pillow comfort

The quieter you become the more you can hear. — BOB RAM DASS

There's something about laying your head on a pillow that instantly evokes feelings of deep, wonderful comfort. Since pillows are so good for the head, it makes sense that they are also perfect for the eyes, hands, feet and neck! Luxurious fabrics coupled with beneficial fillings of flaxseeds and buckwheat hulls make pillows the ultimate relaxation tools.

Go into a room, close the door, put your feet up on a heated *Foot Pillow*, place a *Neck Pillow* around your neck and drape an *Eye, Forehead and Cheek Pillow* over your face. Now breath. Instantly, the problems of the day begin to evaporate, stress starts to fade and calm is restored. After 20 minutes — rejuvenation! Life is good. Now you can face the rest of your day.

## Aromatherapy

Have you ever gone into a department store and been sprayed by perfume sales-people? Some of the scents are quite lovely, while others make you sneeze. The same can be true of aromatherapy. While flaxseeds and buckwheat hulls alone do not generally result in an allergic reaction, certain scents may create one. Pretest by placing a spoonful of crushed botanicals into a small fabric square, tying ends with string and smelling. If you have a reaction, do not use the scents. If the scents make you smile, place a spoonful or two in your pillow.

For resting, lavender is a fine botanical to help you sleep. In addition, you might want to add other favorite scents. I love lemon verbena and pick it fresh from my garden, along with a little sage. I then dry the leaves out on a shelf. Within a week, the moisture has evaporated from the botanicals, leaving them curled and dry. They can then be crushed by hand and placed in a bowl, mixed and spooned into the pillows. You might want to leave some out in a small bowl to place by your bed or on your desk.

The aromatherapy scent will last about 1 year. After that time, simply open up a pillow seam a couple of inches, spoon in a teaspoon or two of fresh botanicals, resew and you're ready for another year of delightful scents.

## A note on fabrics

How do I select a fabric? I prefer silk or prewashed cotton because both are soft. Silk conveys luxury, while cotton communicates comfort. Both hold flaxseed and buckwheat hulls very well. Silk and a natural cotton will cost more than some other fabrics like polyester, but I still prefer the feel.

Fabric stores offer the best variety. Look for fabrics that have tight weaves and, especially with cottons, high thread counts. These fabrics will also work well in the microwave when heating pillows. Buy fabric in $1/2$-yard or 1-yard quantities to save money.

As a side note, the reason for using black fabric on the bottom of facial pillows is because the dark color will help block out light. On an aesthetic note, two-tone pillows provide a nice visual touch.

## A note on sewing and stitches

Sewing by machine is faster, while sewing by hand allows you to do other things at the same time, like talk with friends, watch TV or sit outside.

*on stitches:* Whether by machine or by hand, the stitch should be tight and continuous. Check to make sure that the thread does not pucker. If there is puckering, then the stitch is too tight and you need to sew more loosely. Conversely, make sure the stitches are not too loose. The stitches should lay flat and remain strong and continuous.

### Heating, cooling and storing pillows

Chiropractors, massage therapists and physical therapists know that one way to relax tired muscles is to use warm and chilled packs on aching areas. *Calming Craft* pillows can be used in the same way. The effects can be quite therapeutic. And, at the very least, they feel absolutely wonderful.

By putting a pillow in the microwave for about 6 to 10 minutes, you will have about 20 minutes of warmth.

Placing a pillow in the freezer for about 1 hour will result in about 30 minutes worth of coolness. The pillows will not freeze, but the seeds or hulls retain their chilled properties. Always be sure to place a pillow in a double plastic bag before putting it in the freezer or refrigerator. This will protect against water getting into the pillow. If the pillow becomes wet, the seeds may clump, break down and actually sprout! If the pillow does get wet, quickly place it in the microwave for several minutes to dry. Also, be careful not to place the pillow near food with strong odors. The pillow will absorb food scents.

## Flaxseeds

To the touch, flaxseeds feel almost like liquid. It is that same wonderful effect that makes flaxseeds the perfect filling, particularly for facial pillows. Flaxseeds also act almost like a liquid, filling and contouring the crevices around the eyes, blocking out light, and gently massaging accupressure points around the face. Always make sure the pillow feels comfortable. If it feels the slightest bit uncomfortable, then the pillow is too heavy and you need to remove some flaxseeds.

When placing a flaxseed pillow on the face, allow the seeds to fall into both ends of the pillow, creating a gentle swath across the face. The pillow should lie across the bridge of your nose, with the ends remaining unblocked, so you can breath easily. Flaxseed pillows can be placed in the freezer, refrigerator or microwave or used at room temperature.

## Buckwheat hulls

Did you know that the pillows in Japan's finest hotels are filled with buckwheat hulls? It's true. Buckwheat hull pillows are also found in many Asian homes. For centuries people have known about the wonderful, comforting and therapeutic properties of buckwheat hulls. Buckwheat hulls are resilient and conform to your body. They are also light in weight, have a low density and are completely natural. The hulls are particularly noteworthy for their ability to create a cooling effect. They are able to absorb, transfer and release moisture back out, which creates a cool, comforting feeling while you rest. Buckwheat pillows may be placed in the freezer, refrigerator or microwave or used at room temperature.

When I need a quick 15-minute vacation, without leaving my home or office, I reach for my aromatherapy scented *Eye Pillow*. Within a few moments, my troubles drift away and are replaced with peaceful thoughts. When my mini-vacation ends, I am better able to face the day. Because of the eye pillow's convenient size, it travels exceptionally well from home to office to plane. Place it in a strong plastic bag when traveling.

## Eye Pillow

store cost: $15 to $25

handmade cost: $2 to $6

time: About 30 minutes with a sewing machine, and under 1 hour sewn by hand

### INGREDIENTS (PER PILLOW)

*1 (5-inch x 9-inch) rectangle of colored or patterned heavy silk or heavy cotton fabric*
*1 (5-inch x 9-inch) rectangle of black heavy silk or heavy cotton fabric*
*1 spool black polyester thread*
*8 ounces flaxseeds*

### DIRECTIONS
#### SEWING THE FABRICS BY MACHINE

Each side of the pillow will have a $^1/_2$-inch seam.

1. Place 2 pieces of fabric together and check that both are about the same size.

2. When you look at each piece of fabric, you'll notice that one side looks finished and one side looks dull. Place the finished sides of fabric together so they face inside, and place the dull sides on the outside. If the material has a pattern, place the pattern on the inside.

3. Start with one of the 9-inch sides, place the fabric under a sewing machine needle and measure $^1/_2$ inch from the top and side.

4. Sew from top to bottom, stopping $^1/_2$ inch from the bottom.

5. Turn the fabric toward you so a 5-inch side of the fabric is under the needle, and sew from top to bottom, stopping ¹/₂ inch from the bottom.

6. Turn the fabric toward you so the 9-inch unsewn side of the fabric is under the needle, and sew from top to bottom, stopping ¹/₂ inch from the bottom.

7. Reverse stitch 1 inch from the 5-inch unsewn side, securing the end.

8. On the opposite long side, reverse the stitch 1 inch from the unsewn side, securing the end.

9. Turn the fabric inside out (the finished sides are on the outside and the dull sides are on the inside, and if using a patterned fabric, the pattern is now on the outside) and smooth the fabric flat with hands. You are now ready to fill the pillow.

SEWING THE FABRICS BY HAND

1. Place 2 pieces of fabric together and check that both are about the same size.

2. Look at each piece of fabric and select the side that looks finished, versus the side that looks dull. Place the finished sides of fabric together so they face inside, and place the dull sides on the outside. If the material has a pattern, place the pattern on the inside.

3. Pin two 9-inch sides and one 5-inch side with straight pins ¹/₂ inch around, leaving one short side unpinned.

4. Sew a continuous line ¹/₂ inch from ends of the fabric all the way around, (except for the unpinned 5-inch side).

5. Where the 2 sewn ends meet the unsewn side, stitch an extra 1 inch, securing ends.

6. Turn the fabric inside out (the finished sides are on the outside, the dull sides are on the inside, and if using a patterned fabric, the pattern is now on the outside) and smooth the fabric flat with your hands. You are now ready to fill the pillow.

FILLING THE PILLOW

1. Using a small kitchen scale, measure 8 ounces of flaxseeds.

2. Using a cup, slowly pour the seeds into the opening.

3. Pin the open end and place the pillow over your eyes to see if it feels comfortable. If heavy, remove some seeds. As a rule, 8 ounces or a little less should be fine.

4. Optional: Add 1 tablespoon of lavender seeds or crushed lemon verbena.

SEWING THE OPENING BY MACHINE OR BY HAND

1. Remove pins from the opening, fold ¹/₂ inch on both pieces of fabric inward and press together.

2. Place the needle about ¹/₄ inch from the top and sew across the unsewn side.

There are times when bigger is definitely better. This is true when you've had a really challenging day, your boss has been especially demanding, your kids want your undivided attention, your husband is thinking about switching jobs, your insurance payments will be rising, your washing machine needs to be replaced and your pets are not getting along. Ready to grab aspirin, chocolate or something sharper? Don't! Instead, reach for something softer, like your hand-made *Forehead, Eye and Cheek Pillow*. Larger than your *Eye Pillow*, it nicely covers throbbing temples. The flaxseeds gently hug the pillow across your eyes, uniquely conforming to your face. The sweet smell of lavender lulls you to a gentle rest. The day's troubles begin to fade.

# Forehead, Eye and Cheek Pillow

<u>store cost</u>: $20 to $35

<u>handmade cost</u>: $3 to $7

<u>time</u>: About 30 minutes with a sewing machine, and under 1 hour sewn by hand

## INGREDIENTS (PER PILLOW)

*1 (7-inch x 12-inch) colored or patterned piece of heavy silk or heavy cotton fabric*
*1 (7-inch x 12-inch) black piece of heavy silk or heavy cotton fabric*
*1 spool black polyester thread*
*15 ounces flaxseeds*

## DIRECTIONS
### SEWING THE FABRICS BY MACHINE

Each side of the pillow will have a ¹/₂-inch seam.

1. Place 2 pieces of fabric together and check that both are about the same size.

2. Look at each piece of fabric and select the side that looks more finished, versus the side that looks dull. Place the finished sides of fabric together so they face inside and place the dull sides on the outside. If the material has a pattern, place the pattern on the inside.

3. Start with one of the 12-inch sides, place the fabric under the sewing machine needle and measure ¹/₂ inch from the top and side.

4. Sew from top to bottom, stopping ¹/₂ inch from the bottom.

5. Turn the fabric toward you so a 7-inch side of the fabric is under the needle, and sew from top to bottom, stopping ¹/₂ inch from the bottom.

6. Turn the fabric toward you so the 12-inch unsewn side of the fabric is under the needle, and sew from top to bottom, stopping ¹/₂ inch from the bottom.

7. Reverse stitch 1 inch from the 7-inch unsewn side, securing the end.

8. On the opposite long side, reverse stitch 1 inch from the unsewn side, securing the end.

9. Turn the fabric inside out (the finished sides are on the outside and the dull sides are on the inside, and if using a patterned fabric, the pattern is now on the outside) and smooth the fabric flat with your hands. You are now ready to fill the pillow.

### SEWING THE FABRICS BY HAND

1. Place 2 pieces of fabric together and check that both are about the same size.

2. Check each piece of fabric and select the side that looks more finished from the side that looks dull. Place the finished sides of fabric together so they face inside, and place the dull sides on the outside. If using a material with a pattern, place the clear pattern on the inside.

3. Pin two 12-inch sides and one 7-inch side with straight pins, ½ inch around, leaving one short side unpinned.

4. Sew a continuous line ½ inch from the ends of the fabric all the way around (except for the unpinned 5-inch side).

5. Where the 2 sewn ends meet the unsewn side, stitch an extra 1 inch, securing the ends.

6. Turn the fabric inside out (the finished sides are on the outside, the dull sides are on the inside, and if using a patterned fabric, the pattern is now on the outside) and smooth the fabric flat with your hands. You are now ready to fill the pillow.

### FILLING THE PILLOW

1. Using a small kitchen scale, measure 15 ounces of flaxseeds.

2. Using a cup, slowly pour the seeds into the opening.

3. Pin the open end and place the pillow over your eyes to see if the amount of seeds feels comfortable. If too heavy, remove some of the seeds. As a rule, 15 ounces or less should be fine.

4. Optional: Add 1½ tablespoons of scent, such as lavender seeds and lemon verbena.

### SEWING THE OPENING BY MACHINE OR BY HAND

1. Remove pins from the opening, fold ½ inch on both pieces of fabric inward and press together.

2. Place the needle about ½ inch from the top and sew across the unsewn side.

Some days my neck feels like concrete. My neck is where I tend to hold a lot of stress. Also being hunched over, staring at a computer for a good part of the day doesn't help. To assist in loosening up overstrained muscles, I'll pop my *Neck Pillow* into the microwave for 8 minutes and then wear it around my neck. The warmth permeates my skin, gently telling muscles and ligaments to relax and kneading away stress. The *Neck Pillow* also works well when placed in the freezer and then placed around the neck. Because of its long length, the pillow also helps to relieve tension just below the neck in the upper chest areas.

# Neck Pillow

store cost: $35 to $50

handmade cost: $15 to $20

time: Less than 1 hour with a sewing machine, and about 1½ hours sewn by hand

### INGREDIENTS (PER PILLOW)

*½ yard heavy cotton or cotton fleece fabric in a color or pattern*
*1 spool black polyester thread*
*24 ounces buckwheat hulls*

### DIRECTIONS

This is perhaps the most challenging pillow to make because of its unique U-shape. It may take a few tries to get it right. I know this from experience, so don't become discouraged. With each attempt, your pillow will improve.

### MEASURING AND CUTTING THE FABRICS

1. Using a piece of tracing paper, draw a U-shape that is approximately 9 inches across at the top, 15 inches in the middle, and 14 inches at the bottom. The length is 12 inches.

2. Cut out the U-shape.

3. Place colored or patterned fabric on top of the cutting mat and put the U-shaped piece of tracing paper over the fabric.

4. Using the tracing paper as your guide and working carefully, cut a U-shaped piece of fabric with rotary cutters or scissors.

5. Repeat steps 3 and 4 for the second piece of U-shaped fabric.

### SEWING THE FABRICS BY MACHINE

Each side of the pillow will have a ½-inch seam.

1. Place 2 pieces of fabric together and check to ensure they are both about the same size.

2. Check each piece of fabric and select the side that looks more finished from the side that looks dull. Place the finished sides of fabric together so they face inside, and place the dull sides on the outside. If the material has a pattern, place the pattern on the inside.

3. With a sewing pencil, lightly draw a line ½ inch in from the top of the fabric all the way around the fabric. Repeat this step for the second piece of fabric. This line represents where you will sew.

4. Pin the fabric together all the way around, leaving the opening unpinned.

5. Starting from the top and going to the end, sew along the continuous penciled line. This will take a bit of maneuvering and a slow and steady hand, turning the fabric as you go, except for the unpinned 18-inch side.

6. Reverse stitch 1 inch from the top and bottom of the U-shape, securing the ends.

7. Turn the fabric inside out (the finished sides are on the outside, the dull sides are on the inside, and if using a patterned fabric, the pattern is now on the outside) and smooth the fabric flat with your hands. You are now ready to fill the pillow.

### SEWING THE FABRICS BY HAND

1. Place 2 pieces of fabric together and check to ensure they are both about the same size. Check each piece of fabric and select sides that look more finished and sides that appear dull. Place the finished sides of fabric together so they face inside, and place the dull sides on the outside. If the material has a pattern, place the pattern on the inside.

2. Pin the pieces together all the way around, leaving the opening unpinned.

3. Sew a continuous line 1/2 inch from the ends of the fabric all the way around, except for the unpinned 18-inch side.

4. Where the 2 sewn ends meet the unsewn side, stitch an extra 1 inch, securing the ends.

5. Turn the fabric inside out (the finished sides are on the outside, the dull sides are on the inside, and if using a patterned fabric, the pattern is now on the outside) and smooth the fabric flat with your hands. You are now ready to fill the pillow.

### FILLING THE PILLOW

1. Using a small kitchen scale, measure out 24 ounces of buckwheat hulls.

2. Using a cup, slowly pour the buckwheat hulls into the opening.

3. Pin the open end, sit and rest your head on the pillow to test for comfort. If the pillow feels too firm, remove hulls or, if too spongy, add hulls. Keep adding or removing buckwheat until you have the right feel. You are now ready to sew the opening.

### SEWING THE OPENING BY MACHINE OR BY HAND

1. Remove pins from opening, fold 1/2 inch on both pieces of fabric inward and press together.

2. Place the needle about 1/2 inch from the top and sew across the unsewn side.

This unique pillow works well placed on the floor or on the bed with your feet propped on top of it. With bare feet, luxuriate in the comfort of the buckwheat hulls. With feet on top of the *Foot Pillow*, the hulls almost feel as if they are massaging your soles and toes. Or allow your heels to rest atop the pillow, lifting them into a delightful rest. The pillow may be small in size, but it provides a lot of relief. This pillow can also be brought on an airplane to provide rest for your feet. I keep one on the floor in my office. By placing a plastic bag beneath the pillow you can keep it clean.

# Foot Pillow

<u>store cost</u>: $15 to $35

<u>handmade cost</u>: $4 to $11

<u>time</u>: About 30 minutes with a sewing machine, and under 1 hour sewn by hand

## INGREDIENTS (PER PILLOW)

*2 (10-inch x 12-inch) squares of heavy cotton, nubby cotton, cotton fleece or corduroy fabric in a color or pattern*
*1 spool black polyester thread*
*20 ounces buckwheat hulls*

## DIRECTIONS

### SEWING THE FABRICS BY MACHINE

Each side of the pillow will have a $\frac{1}{2}$-inch seam.

1. Place 2 pieces of fabric together and check to ensure they are both about the same size.

2. Check each piece of fabric and select the side that looks finished from the one that looks dull. Place the finished sides of fabric together so they face inside, and place the dulls sides on the outside. If the material has a pattern, place the pattern on the inside.

3. Start with one of the 12-inch sides, place the fabric under the sewing machine needle and measure $\frac{1}{2}$ inch from the top and side.

4. Sew from top to bottom, stopping $\frac{1}{2}$ inch from the bottom.

5. Turn the fabric toward you so a 10-inch side of the fabric is under the needle, and sew from top to bottom, stopping $\frac{1}{2}$ inch from the bottom.

6. Turn the fabric toward you so the 12-inch unsewn side of the fabric is under the needle, and sew from top to bottom, stopping $\frac{1}{2}$ inch from the bottom.

7. Reverse stitch 1 inch from the 10-inch unsewn side, securing the end.

8. On the opposite long side, reverse stitch 1 inch from the unsewn side, securing the end.

9. Turn the fabric inside out (the finished sides are on the outside, the dull sides are on the inside, and if using a patterned fabric, the pattern is now on the outside) and smooth the fabric flat with your hands. You are now ready to fill the pillow.

### SEWING THE FABRICS BY HAND

1. Place 2 pieces of fabric together and check that both are about the same size.

2. Check each piece of fabric and select the side that looks finished from the one that looks dull. Place the finished sides of fabric together so they face inside, and place the dulls sides on the outside. If the material has a pattern, place the pattern on the inside.

3. Pin the two 12-inch sides and one 10-inch side with straight pins ¼-inch around, leaving one short side unpinned.

4. Sew a continuous line ½ inch from ends of the fabric all the way around (except for the unpinned 10-inch side).

5. Where the 2 sewn ends meet the unsewn side, stitch an extra 1 inch, securing the ends.

6. Turn the fabric inside out (the finished sides are on the outside, the dull sides are on the inside, and if using a patterned fabric, the pattern is now on the outside) and smooth the fabric flat with your hands. You are now ready to fill the pillow.

### FILLING THE PILLOW

1. Using a small kitchen scale, measure 18 ounces of buckwheat hulls.

2. Using a cup, slowly pour the buckwheat hulls into the opening.

3. Pin the open end, sit and rest your feet on the pillow to test for comfort. If the pillow feels too firm, remove hulls or, if too spongy, add hulls. Keep adding and subtracting buckwheat until you obtain the right feel. You are now ready to sew the opening.

### SEWING THE OPENING BY MACHINE OR BY HAND

1. Remove pins from the opening, fold ½ inch on both pieces of fabric inward and press together.

2. Place the needle about ¼ inch from the top and sew across the unsewn side.

## Sleeping Pillow

store cost: $30 to $50

handmade cost: $15 to $20

time: Less than 1 hour with a sewing machine, and about 1½ hours sewn by hand

### INGREDIENTS (PER PILLOW)

*2 (18-inch x 25-inch) squares of heavy cotton or cotton fleece fabric in a color or pattern*
*1 spool black polyester thread*
*5 pounds buckwheat hulls*

### DIRECTIONS
### SEWING THE FABRICS BY MACHINE

Each side of the pillow will have a ½-inch seam.

1. Place 2 pieces of fabric together and check to ensure they are both about the same size.

2. Check each piece of fabric and select the side that looks finished from the one that looks dull. Place the finished sides of fabric together so they face inside, and the dull sides on the outside. If the material has a pattern, place the pattern on the inside.

• • •

*I had used every kind of pillow imaginable in pursuit of a good night's sleep. I tried polyester, foam and goose down, but nothing seemed to provide a comfortable rest. Then I made a* Sleeping Pillow *with buckwheat and instantly felt the difference.*

3. Start with one of the 25-inch sides, place the fabric under the sewing machine needle and measure ½ inch from the top and side.

4. Sew from top to bottom, stopping ½ inch from the bottom.

5. Turn the fabric toward you so an 18-inch side of the fabric is under the needle and sew from top to bottom, stopping ½ inch from the bottom.

6. Turn the fabric toward you so the 25-inch unsewn side of the fabric is under the needle and sew from top to bottom, stopping ½ inch from the bottom.

7. Reverse stitch 1 inch from the 18-inch unsewn side, securing the end.

8. On the opposite long side, reverse stitch 1 inch from the unsewn side, securing the end.

9. Turn the fabric inside out (the finished sides are on the outside, the dull sides are on the inside, and if using a patterned fabric, the pattern is now on the outside) and smooth the fabric flat with your hands. You are now ready to fill the pillow.

### SEWING THE FABRICS BY HAND

1. Place 2 pieces of fabric together and check to ensure that both are about the same size.

2. Check each piece of fabric and select the side that looks finished and the side that looks dull. Place the finished sides of fabric together so they face inside, and place the dull sides on the outside. If the material has a pattern, place the pattern on the inside.

3. Pin the two 25-inch sides and one 18-inch side with straight pins ½-inch around, leaving one short side unpinned.

4. Sew a continuous line ½ inch from ends of the fabric all the way around (except for the unpinned 18-inch side).

5. Where the two sewn ends meet the unsewn side, stitch an extra 1 inch, securing the ends.

6. Turn the fabric inside out (the finished sides are on the outside, the dull sides are on the inside, and if using a patterned fabric, the pattern is now on the outside) and smooth the fabric flat with your hands. You are now ready to fill the pillow.

### FILLING THE PILLOW

1. Using a small kitchen scale, measure out 5 pounds of buckwheat hulls.

2. Using a cup, slowly pour the buckwheat hulls into the opening.

3. Pin the open end and rest your head on the pillow to test for comfort. If the pillow feels too firm, remove hulls or, if too spongy, add hulls. Keep adding and removing buckwheat until you obtain the right feel. You are now ready to sew up the opening.

1. Remove pins from the opening, fold ¹/₂ inch on both pieces of fabric inward and press together.

2. Place the needle about ¹/₄ inch from the top and sew across the unsewn side.

## Chair Pillow

store cost: $20 to $40

handmade cost: $6 to $12

time: About 30 minutes with a sewing machine, and under 1 hour sewn by hand

### INGREDIENTS (PER PILLOW)

*2 (13-inch x 14-inch) squares of heavy cotton, nubby cotton, cotton fleece or*
*    corduroy fabric in a color or pattern*
*1 spool black polyester thread*
*26 ounces buckwheat hulls*

### DIRECTIONS

I find this pillow works well when filled with a good amount of buckwheat hulls. About 26 ounces is perfect for me, but test to see what feels right for you.

### SEWING THE FABRICS BY MACHINE

Each side of the pillow will have a ¹/₂-inch seam.

1. Place 2 pieces of fabric together and check to ensure they are both about the same size.

2. Check each piece of fabric and select the side that looks finished from the side that looks dull. Place the finished sides of fabric together so they face inside, and place the dull sides on the outside. If the material has a pattern, place the pattern on the inside.

3. Start with one of the 14-inch sides, place the fabric under the sewing machine needle and measure ¹/₂ inch from the top and side.

4. Sew from top to bottom, stopping ¹/₂ inch from the bottom.

5. Turn the fabric toward you so a 13-inch side of the fabric is under the needle, and sew from top to bottom, stopping ¹/₂ inch from the bottom.

6. Turn the fabric toward you so the 14-inch unsewn side of the fabric is under the needle, and sew from top to bottom, stopping ¹/₂ inch from the bottom.

7. Reverse stitch 1 inch from the 13-inch unsewn side, securing the end.

8. On the opposite long side, reverse stitch 1 inch from the unsewn side, securing the end.

. . .

Sitting for long periods of time can be uncomfortable. I spend at least four consecutive hours writing a day, and sometimes I don't know which hurts more, my eyes or my bottom. After making a *Chair Pillow*, I found I could sit comfortably for longer periods of time. After you make one, I hope you'll enjoy its benefits as much as I have. The buckwheat hulls gently expand and contract when sitting, and conform to your body, providing a custom fit. Perfect for work or a home office.

9. Turn the fabric inside out (the finished sides are on the outside, the dull sides are on the inside, and if using a patterned fabric, the pattern is now on the outside) and smooth the fabric flat with your hands. You are now ready to fill the pillow.

### SEWING THE FABRICS BY HAND

1. Place 2 pieces of fabric together and check to ensure they are both about the same size.

2. Check each piece of fabric and select the side that looks finished from the one that looks dull. Place the finished sides of fabric together so they face inside, and place the dulls sides on the outside. If the material has a pattern, place the pattern on the inside.

3. Pin the two 14-inch sides and one 13-inch side with straight pins $\frac{1}{2}$-inch around, leaving one short side unpinned.

4. Sew a continuous line $\frac{1}{2}$ inch from ends of the fabric all the way around (except for the unpinned 13-inch side).

5. Where the 2 sewn ends meet the unsewn side, stitch an extra 1 inch, securing the ends.

6. Turn the fabric inside out (the finished sides are on the outside, the dull sides are on the inside, and if using a patterned fabric, the pattern is now on the outside) and smooth the fabric flat with your hands. You are now ready to fill the pillow.

### FILLING THE PILLOW

1. Using a small kitchen scale, measure out 26 ounces of buckwheat hulls.

2. Using a cup, slowly pour the buckwheat hulls into the opening.

3. Pin the open end, sit and rest your head on the pillow to test for comfort. If the pillow feels too firm, remove hulls or, if too spongy, add hulls. Keep adding and removing buckwheat until you have the right feel. You are now ready to sew the opening.

### SEWING THE OPENING BY MACHINE OR BY HAND

1. Remove pins from the opening, fold $\frac{1}{2}$ inch on both pieces of fabric inward and press together.

2. Place the needle about $\frac{1}{4}$ inch from the top and sew across the unsewn side.

# Versatile Pillow

store cost: $20 to $40

handmade cost: $6 to $12

time: About 30 minutes with a sewing machine, under 1 hour sewn by hand

INGREDIENTS (PER PILLOW)

2 (15-inch x 17-inch) squares of heavy cotton, nubby cotton or cotton fleece fabric
   in a color or pattern
1 spool black polyester thread
24 ounces buckwheat hulls

DIRECTIONS

SEWING THE FABRICS BY MACHINE

Each side of the pillow will have a ¹/₂-inch seam.

1. Place 2 pieces of fabric together and check to ensure they are both about the same size. Check each piece of fabric and select the side that looks finished from the side that looks dull. Place the finished sides of fabric together so they face inside, and place the dull sides on the outside. If the material has a pattern, place the pattern on the inside.

2. Start with one of the 17-inch sides, place the fabric under the sewing machine needle and measure ¹/₂ inch from the top and side.

3. Sew from top to bottom, stopping ¹/₂ inch from the bottom.

4. Turn the fabric toward you so a 15-inch side of the fabric is under the needle, and sew from top to bottom, stopping ¹/₂ inch from the bottom.

5. Turn the fabric toward you so the 17-inch unsewn side of the fabric is under the needle, and sew from top to bottom, stopping ¹/₂ inch from the bottom.

6. Reverse stitch 1 inch from the 15-inch unsewn side, securing the end.

7. On the opposite long side, reverse stitch 1 inch from the unsewn side, securing the end.

8. Turn the fabric inside out (the finished sides are on the outside and the dull sides are on the inside, and if using a patterned fabric, the pattern is now on the outside) and smooth the fabric flat with your hands. You are now ready to fill the pillow.

SEWING THE FABRICS BY HAND

1. Place 2 pieces of fabric together and check to ensure they are both about the same size.

2. Check that each piece of fabric is about the same size, and then select the side that looks finished from the side that looks dull. Place the finished sides of fabric together so they face inside, and place the dull side on the outside. If the material has a pattern, place the pattern on the inside.

I call this the *Versatile Pillow* because it's the perfect size for all of your rest and relaxation needs. The pillow is a great size to use while sitting on a plane, or just lying on the couch. This pillow provides comfort for your head or feet. You can also use it when you go on a long road trip to relieve fatigue from sitting too long. Wrap it in a large plastic bag, and you can use it outdoors for sports events, sitting in the park or at a picnic.

3. Pin the two 17-inch sides and one 15-inch side with straight pins ¼-inch around, leaving one short side unpinned.

4. Sew a continuous line ½ inch from ends of fabric all the way around (except for the unpinned 15-inch side).

5. Where the 2 sewn ends meet the unsewn side, stitch an extra 1 inch, securing the ends.

6. Turn the fabric inside out (the finished sides are on the outside, the dull sides are on the inside, and if using a patterned fabric, the pattern is now on the outside) and smooth the fabric flat with your hands. You are now ready to fill the pillow.

### FILLING THE PILLOW

1. Using a small kitchen scale, measure out 24 ounces of buckwheat hulls.

2. Using a cup, slowly pour the buckwheat hulls into the opening.

3. Pin the open end, sit and rest your head on the pillow to test for comfort. If the pillow feels too firm, remove hulls or, if too spongy, add hulls. Keep adding and removing buckwheat until you have the right feel. You are now ready to sew the opening.

### SEWING THE OPENING BY MACHINE OR BY HAND

1. Remove pins from the opening, fold ½ inch inward on both pieces of fabric and press together.

2. Place the needle about ¼ inch from the top and sew across the unsewn side.

## Computer Keyboard Pillow

store cost: $15 to $30

handmade cost: $4 to $11

time: Less than 30 minutes with a sewing machine, and under 1 hour sewn by hand

### INGREDIENTS (PER PILLOW)

*2 (4½-inch x 19-inch) rectangles of heavy cotton, nubby cotton, cotton fleece or corduroy fabric in a color or pattern*
*1 spool black polyester thread*
*16 ounces flaxseeds*

### DIRECTIONS
### SEWING THE FABRICS BY MACHINE

Each side of the pillow will have a ½-inch seam.

1. Place 2 pieces of fabric together and check that both are about the same size.

· · ·

People are spending more time at their computers. Maladies can often result, including carpal tunnel syndrome and other wrist and arm afflictions. To give wrists a rest, try making a *Computer Keyboard Pillow*. The consistency of flaxseeds gives, responding to wrist movement and providing a gentle cushion for the quick hand movements of typing. I chose a fun cow-patterned fabric, which brings smiles and makes the pillow a fabulous conversation piece as well as a wonderful, inexpensive gift.

2. Check each piece of fabric and select sides that look finished and sides that look dull. Place the finished sides of fabric together so they face inside, and the dull sides on the outside. If the material has a pattern, place the pattern on the inside.

3. Start with one of the 19-inch sides, place the fabric under the sewing machine needle and measure $1/2$ inch from the top and side.

4. Sew from top to bottom, stopping $1/2$ inch from the bottom.

5. Turn the fabric toward you so a $4^1/2$-inch side of the fabric is under the needle and sew from top to bottom, stopping $1/2$ inch from the bottom.

6. Turn the fabric toward you so the 19-inch unsewn side of the fabric is under the needle, and sew from top to bottom, stopping $1/2$ inch from the bottom.

7. Reverse stitch 1 inch from the $4^1/2$-inch unsewn side, securing the end.

8. On opposite long side, reverse stitch 1 inch from the unsewn side, securing the end.

9. Turn the fabric inside out (the finished sides are on the outside, the dull sides are on the inside, and if using a patterned fabric, the pattern is on the outside) and smooth the fabric flat with your hands. You are now ready to fill the pillow.

### SEWING THE FABRICS BY HAND

1. Place 2 pieces of fabric together and check to ensure they are both about the same size.

2. Check each piece of fabric and select the side that looks finished from the one that looks dull. Place the finished sides of fabric together so they face inside, and place the dulls sides on the outside. If the material has a pattern, place the pattern on the inside.

3. Pin the two 19-inch sides and one $4^1/2$-inch side with straight pins, $1/2$-inch around, leaving one short side unpinned.

4. Sew a continuous line $1/2$ inch from the ends of the fabric all the way around, (except for the unpinned $4^1/2$-inch side).

5. Where the 2 sewn ends meet the unsewn side, stitch an extra 1 inch, securing the ends.

6. Turn the fabric inside out (the finished sides are on the outside, the dull sides are on the inside, and if using a patterned fabric, the pattern is now on the outside) and smooth the fabric flat with your hands. You are now ready to fill the pillow.

### FILLING THE PILLOW

1. Using a small kitchen scale, measure out 16 ounces of flaxseeds.

2. Use a cup to slowly pour the flaxseeds into the opening.

3. Pin the open end and rest your wrists on it to test for comfort. If the pillow feels too firm, remove seeds or, if too spongy, add seeds. Keep adding and removing seeds until you obtain the right feel. You are now ready to sew the opening.

1. Remove the pins from the opening, fold $1/2$ inch on both pieces of fabric inward and press together.

2. Place the needle about $1/4$ inch from the top and sew across the unsewn side.

## Computer Mouse Pillow

<u>store cost</u>: $10 to $20

<u>handmade cost</u>: $2 to $7

<u>time</u>: About 15 minutes with a sewing machine, and under 30 minutes sewn by hand

### INGREDIENTS (PER PILLOW)

2 ($4^{1}/_{2}$-inch x 5-inch) squares heavy cotton, nubby cotton, cotton fleece or corduroy
fabric in a solid color or pattern
1 spool black polyester thread
4 ounces flaxseeds

### DIRECTIONS
### SEWING THE FABRICS BY MACHINE

Each side of the pillow will have a $1/2$-inch seam.

1. Place 2 pieces of fabric together and check that both are about the same size.

2. Check each piece of fabric and select sides that look finished from sides than look dull. Place the finished sides of fabric together so they face inside, and the dull sides on the outside. If the material has a pattern, place the pattern on the inside.

3. Start with one of the 5-inch sides, place the fabric under the sewing machine needle and measure $1/2$ inch from the top and side.

4. Sew from top to bottom, stopping $1/2$ inch from the bottom.

5. Turn the fabric toward you so a $4^{1}/_{2}$-inch side of the fabric is under the needle, and sew from top to bottom, stopping $1/2$ inch from the bottom.

6. Turn the fabric toward you so the 5-inch unsewn side of the fabric is under the needle, and sew from top to bottom, stopping $1/2$ inch from the bottom.

7. Reverse stitch 1 inch from the $4^{1}/_{2}$-inch unsewn side, securing the end.

8. On the opposite long side, reverse stitch 1 inch from the unsewn side, securing the end.

9. Turn the fabric inside out (the finished sides are on the outside, the dull sides are on the inside, and if using a patterned fabric, the pattern is now on the outside) and smooth the fabric flat with your hands. You are now ready to fill the pillow.

I firmly believe people were not meant to be moving a mouse around all day with one of their hands. It's unnatural. A mouse pillow provides a comfy cushion for your wrist, giving it a more realistic sweep of motion. I swear by this pillow and so do friends and family that I've given it to as gifts. This is a truly terrific low cost, high impact gift that makes a wonderful companion gift with the keyboard pillow.

### SEWING THE FABRICS BY HAND

1. Place 2 pieces of fabric together and check to ensure they are both about the same size.

2. Check each piece of fabric and select the side that looks finished from the one that looks dull. Place the finished sides of fabric together so they face inside, and place the dulls sides on the outside. If the material has a pattern, place the pattern on the inside.

3. Pin the two 5-inch sides and one 4$\frac{1}{2}$-inch side with straight pins, $\frac{1}{4}$-inch around, leaving one short side unpinned.

4. Sew a continuous line $\frac{1}{2}$ inch from ends of fabric all the way around (except for the unpinned 4$\frac{1}{2}$-inch side).

5. Where the 2 sewn ends meet the unsewn side, stitch an extra 1 inch, securing the ends.

6. Turn the fabric inside out (the finished sides are on the outside, the dull sides are on the inside, and if using a patterned fabric, the pattern is now on the outside) and smooth the fabric flat with your hands. You are now ready to fill the pillow.

### FILLING THE PILLOW

1. Using a small kitchen scale, measure out 4 ounces of flaxseeds.

2. Using a cup, slowly pour the flaxseeds into the opening.

3. Pin the open end, sit and rest your hand on the pillow to test for comfort. If the pillow feels too firm, remove seeds or, if too spongy, add seeds. Keep adding and removing seeds until you obtain the right feel. You are now ready to sew up the opening.

### SEWING THE OPENING BY MACHINE OR BY HAND

1. Remove the pins from the opening, fold $\frac{1}{2}$ inch on both pieces of fabric inward and press together.

2. Place the needle about $\frac{1}{4}$ inch from the top and sew across the unsewn side.

## ✳ Notes and Ideas

* * *

___ * * * ___

___ * * * ___

# fountains

There is no end. There is no beginning.
There is only the infinite passion of life.
— FEDERICO FELLINI

The sound of flowing waters is nature's music. Do you find yourself hoping to encounter a river or a stream when you go hiking? I do. I love to sit near the water and listen to its gentle, running sound. The ambient sounds of water gently soothe and intrinsically renew our spirits. Unfortunately, you can't always hike nature's paths to hear the cadences of the wonderful waters, but you can do the next best thing. Bring the outdoor, rhythmic resonance of a river or a stream indoors by making your own tabletop fountain. These fascinating fountains bring the soothing sounds indoors to create a calm and relaxing environment at home or work.

I bought my first waterfall at an outdoor fair and immediately fell in love with it, but not its price — $200! I negotiated it down to $150, still quite a lot of money. When I got home and put the fountain together, I saw that the components were really very basic and the entire fountain could not have cost more than $30 to make. Out of curiosity, I started visiting garden centers. I'd inspect the fountains and slowly I began to decipher the ingredients needed to make one. I saw ways to build up rocks around necessary hardware, such as a pump, so only the aesthetic components showed.

I saw that you don't have to spend a lot of money on accent pieces. Items that you may have at home or can easily find, such as glass, shells and flowers, can be used. The vessel, the base that holds the pump and water, need not be expensive. In fact, I'll show you how to transform an old gardening pot into a beautiful fountain.

You'll also find that waterfalls are very easy to make and can be created to reflect different tastes and fit into every conceivable decor.

There are few pursuits as satisfying as making something with your own hands. There are few things as enriching as doing something creative. There are few sounds in life that touch us on a visceral level — and running water is one of them.

Indoor fountains are the perfect antidotes to busy homes and stressful offices. Before I turn on my computer, I plug in my fountain. In the face of deadlines, the waterfall has helped keep my sanity up and my stress level down.

Making fountains is a lot of fun and while safe, you are working with water and electricity, so use caution. Never insert a wet plug into an electrical outlet. If it's wet, wipe it dry and then plug the cord in. You can also create a "dew loop" in the cord. This will likely eliminate water from reaching the electrical outlet. To create a dew loop, you need an outlet positioned in the wall so that the cord goes down toward the ground, and then loops upward into the wall outlet. This means that the water is unlikely to go into the outlet because it would have to go down and then up, which gravity would prevent.

## Vessels

Use bowls, flowerpots or wide dishes you already own, or buy them at a discount store, a flea market or a tag sale. Every vessel you choose must have a completely flat bottom so the fountain will not tilt and will sit securely. If you want to use a more pricey vessel, by all means do.

The containers can be ceramic, clay, glass or plastic. The key is to ensure that the ceramic or clay vessel is waterproof. To test a container, fill it with water, place a dish or bowl underneath, and set it aside for a day. If you find water at the bottom of the bowl or dish, then the main bowl leaks. To repair leaks, visit your local hardware store and purchase a waterproof sealant. When using sealant, apply a coat, let it dry, apply a second coat and continue until you have painted four to five layers.

After fully sealing, test with water again. If the bottom container is dry, proceed. If it still leaks, apply several more coats and retest.

Glass or plastic vessels do not need testing. However, if they have cracks, do not use them for a fountain.

## The vessel as canvas

When deciding on your vessel, think what role you want it to play in the overall look of your fountain. Think of the vessel as a blank canvas on which you are going to create a painting. The canvas is the background for the colors and the image that will be revealed. The same is true for a fountain. Often the true look and personality of a fountain is revealed through its accent pieces, rather than its vessel.

## The pump

What drives the fountain is its submersible pump. These small, no more than 2-inch x 2-inch x 1½-inch pumps are actually quite powerful. Most often used in aquariums, these pumps are equally efficient in a water fountain. They cost about $20 to $40 and are available in garden centers, aquarium stores and some hardware stores.

The motor is hermetically sealed and live electrical parts are immersed in a protective epoxy resin to provide insulation against water damage and electric shock. As a result, the pump may be totally submersed without affecting its operation. The motor is extremely compact, energy-efficient and usually maintenance-free. It produces a power-ful, continuous output of water.

A pump generally has small suction cups on the bottom that keep it in place and a water intake valve for filtration. Most important is the water volume, which you can control by sliding it either up or down for low to maximum pressure. The amount of water coming through the pump will impact the sound of the water.

The energy consumption of a pump is generally quite low, giving off perhaps 5 watts of electricity, which monetarily translates to pennies a day to run.

## Pump cleaning

A well-maintained pump will last for years, if properly cared for during use. Submers-ible pumps are very easy to clean. Simply pull out the face front, and you will find the pump's motor, which resembles a small rudder. Using cotton swabs and a mixture of vinegar and hot water, remove crystal sediments, buildup and any gunk that may have accumulated. Also wash the filter, if included, under running water. After removing sediments, soak the motor and the rest of the housing in vinegar and hot water. Clean bimonthly or sooner if the pump sounds strained, to ensure its longevity.

## Water

If the tap water in your area is soft, then it is perfectly fine to use in a fountain. If you have hard water, it is better to use bottled spring or distilled water. Hard water will add to mineral crystal buildup in your fountain, while soft water will not.

accents
to capture your
imagination

## Water evaporation

Since the reservoirs of water fountains tend to be small, water will evaporate quickly. Climate and humidity will also impact evaporation. Check the water level of your fountain on a daily basis. At all times the pump should be fully submersed. If the water level doesn't cover the pump, it needs to be immediately filled. Allowing the pump to run without enough water can damage it. You'll hear a groaning sound from the pump if the reservoir needs to be filled. Always check the water level first before plugging in the pump.

## Tubing

This is an important fountain element as it carries the water from the pump's spout to the surface. Tubing is available in hard and soft form, and thin-walled or thick-walled. Soft tubing is more flexible, while hard tubing is more rigid. In many instances thick-walled hard tubing is preferred, as its stiffness is better suited for directing water upward. Tubing is amazingly inexpensive, as low as 33¢ a foot. Splurge and buy three feet for under $1 so you can experiment with different sizes. You can find tubing at hardware stores, garden centers or aquarium stores. Clerks at the stores will cut tubing to size for you, or you can cut it yourself with strong, sharp scissors. If you want to snake the tubing around rocks and other accents, then soft tubing is better.

How much tubing should you use? It depends on the depth of the bowl and how high you want the water to flow. If you have a shallow bowl, 2 inches of tubing is probably enough. If your bowl has greater depth, then you will likely want more tubing. Measure to be sure of the length you will need. Each pump has a different water-height capacity, so check the directions.

## Accents

This is where you can be truly creative. The accent pieces such as rocks, slate, shells, glass, flowers, candles and more make a fountain unique. When choosing accents, think in terms of looks, sounds and how you want the water to flow. You can find rocks and slate at garden centers and aquarium stores. At the latter store, many of the accents used for aquariums can also be used in fountains. Look for larger rocks that have holes in them and can be placed over tubing. Think about color, size and the overall look of your fountain. Buy accents that interest you, and create as you go along. For variety, buy slate, sandstone, glass rocks, shells and whatever else captures your imagination.

## Beware of blocking a pump's intake valve

A common mistake that beginning fountain creators make is to arrange rocks directly against the intake valve of the pump. Doing so inhibits the air space around the valve, resulting in a gurgling sound from the pump as it tries to suck in water. If blocked, the pump will not receive an adequate supply of water and can be damaged. Remember to build rocks around the pump and never block the intake valve.

# General Materials and Tools

*vessel*

*submersible pump*

*tubing*

*water*

*accent pieces*

*1 pair of scissors*

*1 roll paper towels*

*several cloth towels*

*1 meat baster*

*1 bottle E6000 glue*

*1 bottle waterproof sealant*

*1 tube epoxy putty*

*1 tube waterproof epoxy glue*

*1 package modeling clay*

## Basic Fountain: Main Directions

The following directions are to be used as the main directions for all the fountain recipes that follow. When needed, specific directions will be included for each fountain. Consult the master directions before assembling fountains with specific directions.

store cost: $50 to $100

handmade cost: $30 for the pump. By using a bowl you already own, and stones you collect at the beach or around your yard, you shouldn't have to spend any money.

time: 30 minutes to 1 hour

### DIRECTIONS

1. On a kitchen table or counter, place a layer of paper towels to absorb water that may splash from the fountain.

2. Be sure that you can plug the cord from the pump into a nearby electrical outlet.

3. Clean and dry the bowl and accents, and place them along with the pump and tubing on the table. Put the pump in the middle of the bowl.

4. Press firmly so the pump's suction-cup feet stick to the bottom of the bowl.

5. Place the desired length of tubing over the spout so it fits snugly.

6. Set the water volume of the pump on low.

7. Fill the bowl with water so that the intake valve of the pump and pump are fully submersed.

8. Plug the pump into a grounded wall outlet. There may be some splashing and gurgling from the pump. Unplug and replug several times until you hear an even sound of water.

9. Place rocks around and against the pump. Whenever you build a fountain, you will always want to first build up and around the pump. This lays the groundwork for placing specialty and focal items on top.

10. Choose a focal point and build around it. It may be a large rock, a piece of quartz, a ceramic animal, chimes or even a candle. Choose items that are important to you. A fountain can be purely decorative, symbolic or perhaps a bit of both. This is where your creativity really comes into play. Arrange accent pieces so they are appealing to your eye. Rearrange stones until you have the look you desire.

11. Next, experiment with water sounds. A fountain is a combination of visual aesthetics and the sound of running water. Raise the water volume. Move the rocks around. Use the meat baster to remove water. Listen to the sound. Does it need more water or less? What looks and sounds the best? Move the stones in a different direction and you will hear a different sound. Find the arrangement that produces the sounds that are most appealing to you.

## Shell Fountain

store cost: $75 to $150

handmade cost: $30 for the pump and tubing. If using your own shells, rocks and bowl, there will be no additional costs. If purchasing some or all of the additional ingredients new, add another $20 to $30. If purchasing some or all of the additional ingredients used at flea markets, add around $5 to $10.

time: Less than 1 hour

SPECIAL INGREDIENTS
[ If choosing a 7-inch bowl, use shells no more than 4 inches. The shells can be larger if the bowl is longer. ]
1 (7-inch x 10-inch) vessel or bowl
3 (4-inch x 7-inch) large shells, small shells and rocks
1 tube E6000 glue

SPECIAL DIRECTIONS
1. Build stones and smaller shells around the pump and inside the vessel.

2. Use E6000 to glue shells on top of each other, but in a stepped, cantilevered fashion so the water will flow from one shell into the other.

3. Position shells next to the pump's spout. If they can be secured with rocks, do so. Otherwise, unplug the pump, dry off rocks you wish to place shells on, dry the shells and glue them to rocks. Allow the glue to dry. Replug the cord. Watch the water flow.

• • •

Large shells form the focal point of this aesthetic fountain. From the pump's spout, the water flows down into the first shell, where it collects; runs over into the second shell, where it accumulates; and flows into the third shell, where it pools to the bottom of the bowl.

Thin sheets of black slate against a colored vessel create a modern, yet natural fountain. The look is stark, minimal and reminiscent of the outdoors. Because the stones are black, they will match any decor.

This is a beautiful way to make a fountain because the stones, when placed one on top of the other, resemble a sculpture. The tubing holds the stones in place so there is no need for glue.

## Slate Fountain

store cost: $75 to $150

handmade cost: $30 for the pump and tubing. Add $10 to $20 for the slate. The rocks can be found on the beach or elsewhere.

time: Less than 1 hour

### SPECIAL INGREDIENTS

The size of the slate depends on the size of your vessel, so measure the length of your vessel and buy slate that can cover the opening, along with several smaller pieces for accent.

*1 (7-inch x 10-inch) vessel or bowl*
*2 to 3 pieces of thin black slate*
*10 to 20 heavy square rocks*

### SPECIAL DIRECTIONS

1. Lean larger square rocks against the pump.

2. Place stones around the bowl, using the slate as the top pieces.

## Stacked Stone Fountain

store cost: $75 to $150

handmade cost: $30 for the pump and tubing. Add up to $20 for the stones.

time: Less than 1 hour

### SPECIAL INGREDIENTS

[ Sandstone or lava rocks can be purchased from aquarium stores and pet stores. ]
*1 (4-inch to 5-inch length) tubing*
*3 to 4 sandstones or lava rocks with holes in the middle or side*
  *accent stones*

### SPECIAL DIRECTIONS

1. Build stones around the pump.

2. Stack sandstones around tubing until they reach the top of the tube.

3. Turn the pump on.

# Copper Tubing Fountain

store cost: $60 to $100

handmade cost: $30 for the pump and tubing. Add another $1 to $2 for the copper joint. Use found accent pieces and bowl to save money.

time: Less than 1 hour

SPECIAL INGREDIENTS

*1 small T-shaped or curved copper joint*

SPECIAL DIRECTIONS

1. Arrange accent pieces around the pump in the vessel.

2. Fit a copper joint over the tubing spout.

3. Experiment with the water level to attain the desired sound.

# Flowerpot Fountain

store cost: $50 to $75

handmade cost: $30 for the pump and tubing. Add another $1 or $2 for the epoxy. Use a flowerpot you already own and accent pieces to create this fountain.

time: Less than 1 hour

SPECIAL INGREDIENTS

*1 beloved flowerpot*
*1 bottle waterproof epoxy*

SPECIAL DIRECTIONS

1. Completely mix the resin and a hardening agent to form an epoxy paste.

2. Fill the flowerpot hole.

3. Allow the resin to dry overnight.

4. Test for leakage by filling the pot with water.

5. If it leaks, apply another layer of the combined agents and allow the resin to dry; retest.

6. If there is no leakage, build your fountain.

• • •

Copper joints are a wonderful addition to a fountain. The joints, which are T-shaped or curved, fit over and cover the top of the tubing spout. The water has a top surface and shoots out of both sides of the T-joint. At the curved joint, the water comes out of one side. Over time, the water will give the copper a beautiful green patina.

• • •

Find a favorite flowerpot and use it to make a fountain. But there's a problem — the pot, like most flowerpots, has a drainage hole on its bottom side. Read the directions below and you can learn how to turn a pot into a great fountain!

This is a folksy fountain that works equally well on a table at home or on your desk at the office. By placing the fountain in the basket, it is like putting a picture into a frame. Choose a basket that you like, so the basket hides the vessel. The look of the bowl is secondary to the look of the basket, so find one that you love.

## Fountain in a Basket

store cost: $75 to $150

handmade cost: $30 for the pump and tubing. Add another $1 to $5 for a basket that you purchase at a flea market.

time: Less than 1 hour

SPECIAL INGREDIENTS
*1 basket*
*1 roll plastic wrap*

SPECIAL DIRECTIONS

1. Build your fountain.

2. Line the basket with plastic.

3. Place the fountain in the basket.

# ✳ Notes and Ideas

* * *

* * *

# Suppliers Resource List

Many of the *Calming Craft* ingredients can be purchased in grocery, health food and hardware stores as well hobby and craft shops. Here is a list of suppliers for your convenience.

### CANDLES

**Yaley Enterprises**
7664 Avianca Drive
Redding, CA 96002
Phone: 800.959.2539 or 530.365.2525
Website: www.yaley.com

### GLYCERIN SOAPS

Websites: www.ebarge.com
www.craftpals.org
www.eti-usa
www.essentialessences.com

### POTPOURRI

**San Francisco Herb Co.**
250 14th Street
San Francisco, CA 94103
Phone: 800.227.4530 or 415.861.7174
Fax: 415.861.4440
Website: www.sfherb.com

### PILLOWS

**James Farrell & Co.**
(for buckwheat hulls and flaxseeds)
506 Second Avenue, 31st Floor
Seattle, WA 98104
Phone: 206.623.1993
Fax: 206.623.5396

### FOUNTAINS

**FountainHeads**
1827 Scott Street
San Francisco, CA 94115
Phone: 415.921.7902

# Index

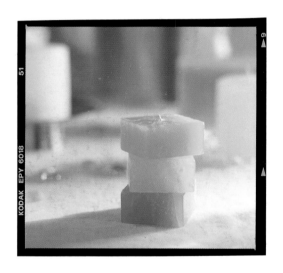